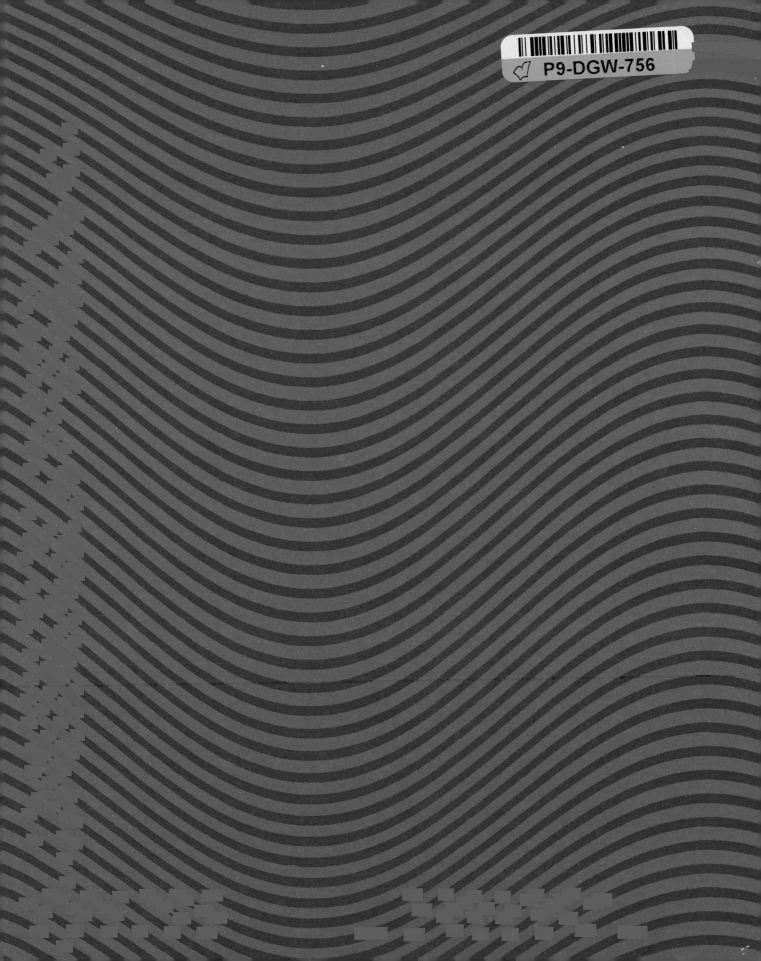

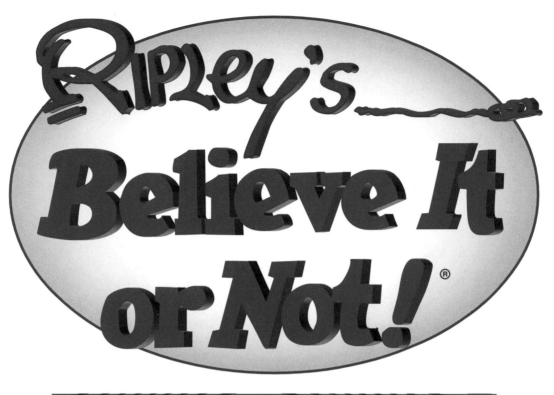

SPECIAL EDITION

By Mary Packard
and the Editors of Ripley Entertainment

Illustrations by
Leanne Franson

SCHOLASTIC INC.

New York   Toronto   London   Auckland   Sydney

Mexico City   New Delhi   Hong Kong   Buenos Aires

Library of Congress Cataloging-in-Publication Data
Packard, Mary.
    Ripley's believe it or not! / by Mary Packard and the editors of
Ripley Entertainment ; illustrations by Leanne Franson.—Special ed.
        p. cm.
Includes index.
    ISBN 0-439-26040-X — ISBN 0-439-26041-8 (pbk.)
    1. Curiosities and wonders—Juvenile literature. [1. Curiosities and
wonders.] I. Franson, Leanne, ill. II. Ripley Entertainment Inc.
III. Title.
    AG243 .P24 2001   031. 02—dc21   2001020936

Developed by Nancy Hall, Inc.
Designed by Atif Toor
Cover Design by Louise Bova
Photo research by Laura Miller

12 11 10 9 8 7 6 5 4 3 2 1   1 2 3 4 5 6 / 0

Printed in Singapore
First Scholastic printing, September 2001

CONTENTS

MEET MR. RIPLEY

obert Ripley was born on Christmas Day in 1890 in Santa Rosa, California. Young Robert showed artistic talent from the start, and by the time he was 14, he had already sold one of his drawings to *Life* (an early magazine unrelated to today's *LIFE*). He was also a natural athlete who hoped for a career in baseball. But Ripley's dreams of pitching in the big leagues were shattered at the age of 15 when he broke his arm playing in his first professional game.

No doubt this was a terrible blow to him. But as it turned out, the accident was a stroke of good luck. He was forced to return to his earlier goal of becoming a professional artist, and when he signed on as sports cartoonist for the *New York Globe,* he was able to combine his two passions, drawing and sports, in one job. One day, as he sat staring at the blank piece of paper on his desk, the ideas just weren't coming. Finally, in desperation, the young cartoonist created an altogether different kind of comic strip. He put together a group of assorted athletic facts and feats from his personal files and, though he didn't think much of it, he handed it in to his editor. The next morning, Ripley was greeted at the door by his publisher. "Can you come up with more strips like the one you drew yesterday?" the publisher asked. "Our readers are clamoring for them!"

> **❝ I venture to say that I've been called a liar more than anyone else in the world. I enjoy being called a liar. I don't blame anyone for thinking me one, because there's nothing stranger than the truth. ❞**
>
> **—Robert Ripley**

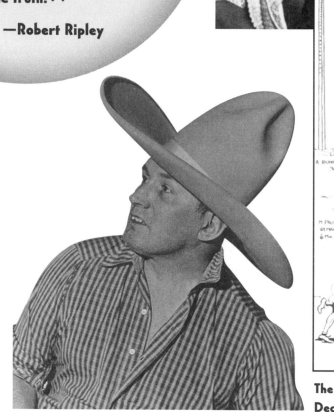

The first Believe It or Not! cartoon, published December 19, 1918.

So it was purely by accident that Ripley became an overnight sensation—a pretty good Believe It or Not story in itself.

By 1922 his column was syndicated. It didn't take long for his readership to reach 80 million, and Ripley became the first millionaire cartoonist in history. Ripley quickly realized that Believe It or Nots could be found in all walks of life, and so he expanded his column to include them. Not even a man of Ripley's monumental imagination could have foreseen what adventures his career would bring. In his search for the unbelievable, he made extensive trips around the world and visited places few people had ever heard of, from the Temple of Heaven in China to a town in Norway named Hell. On one trip alone, he crossed two continents, covering 24,000 miles—1,000 of them by donkey, horse, and camel. Each of Mr. Ripley's excursions contributed new and awesome wonders that he added to his syndicated features.

- Robert Ripley was the first person to broadcast to every nation in the world simultaneously, with the help of translators who delivered his messages in various languages.

- The "Indiana Jones" of his time, Robert Ripley visited a total of 201 countries, traveling a distance equal to 18 complete trips around the world.

- Ripley owned one of the largest and most expensive collections of automobiles in the world, but he never learned to drive.

- Many people wrote to Ripley, hoping he would use their ideas in a Believe It or Not! In 1937, the young Charles Schulz was first published when he sent in a cartoon about the ability of his dog, Sparky, to eat pins, tacks, screws, and razor blades. Sparky is the same dog that later served as the model for Snoopy, in Schulz's world-famous comic strip, *Peanuts*.

Just about everything Ripley touched seemed to turn to gold. When he was persuaded to publish his cartoons in book form, each became a best-seller. In 1930, his Believe It or Nots! were featured on a radio show called *The Collier Hour*. These segments were so successful that Ripley launched a radio show of his own. In the 1940s, Ripley moved into the fledgling television industry. The popularity of his radio show gave him a ready-made audience,

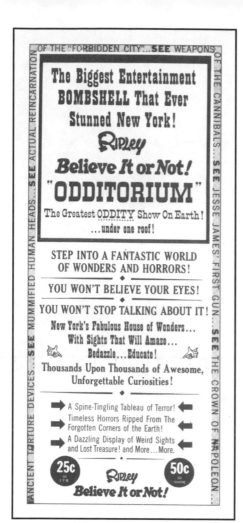

and the TV show was an instant success. At the 1933 Century of Progress World's Fair in Chicago, Ripley opened his first Odditorium, a museum of the fascinating and bizarre. More than two million people passed through its doors, making it one of the most popular attractions at the exposition. People fainted at the sight of contortionists, magicians, eye-poppers, and razor-blade eaters, but that did not stop Ripley from opening other Odditoriums around the country. Ripley delighted in proving that real life in all its variety can be stranger and more wonderful than fiction. Although he was often called the "world's biggest liar," one of the more enduring legacies left by Robert Ripley would be his insistence on the authentication and verification of the facts presented in his cartoons. "I venture to say that I've been called a liar more than anyone else in the world," said Ripley. "I enjoy being called a liar. I don't blame anyone for thinking me one, because there's nothing stranger than the truth."

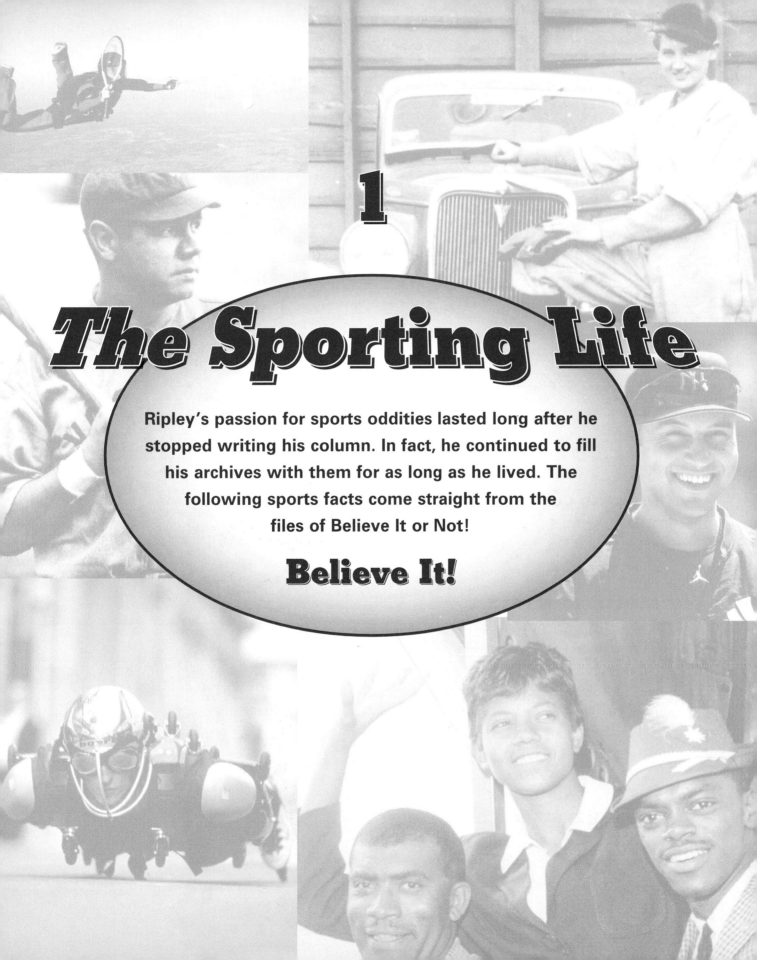

1

The Sporting Life

Ripley's passion for sports oddities lasted long after he stopped writing his column. In fact, he continued to fill his archives with them for as long as he lived. The following sports facts come straight from the files of Believe It or Not!

Believe It!

THEY SAID IT COULDN'T BE DONE

MAMA KNOWS BEST: Boxer Egerton Marcus, an Olympic middleweight medalist, learned his skills in the ring from his mother, a 45-year-old former welterweight.

THE MAN: In February 1927, Babe Ruth (below) hit 125 home runs in one hour in an exhibition game at Wrigley Field, Los Angeles, California.

DIAMOND GIRL: In 1931, Jackie Mitchell (above), the first woman to play professional baseball, struck out Babe Ruth and Lou Gehrig in six straight pitches.

SOMETHING IN THE AIR: No one knows why a tiny impoverished town like San Pedro de Macoris in the Dominican Republic produces so many Major League players. But professional scouts really don't care what the reason is. They'll continue to make the trek, just as long as they keep discovering talent like Sammy Sosa, George Bell, Pedro Guerrerro, and Tony Fernandez.

PITCHER PERFECT: In 1956, Don Larsen of the New York Yankees pitched the only perfect game ever in a World Series.

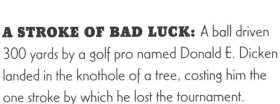

THE FOOTBALL DIET:
In 1937, Bill Mattis (right), a Tulane University halfback, lost 20.5 pounds in a single football game.

A STROKE OF BAD LUCK: A ball driven 300 yards by a golf pro named Donald E. Dicken landed in the knothole of a tree, costing him the one stroke by which he lost the tournament.

HORSING AROUND: Jonathan James Toogood, a 19th-century equestrian from Overblow, England, regularly jumped hedges while riding backward.

TRIPLE THREAT: In 1938, boxer Henry "Homicide Hank" Armstrong (above) held all three weight divisional world boxing titles at the same time.

A WOMAN'S TOUCH: Hessie Donahue, a 19th-century female boxer, once knocked out heavyweight champion, John L. Sullivan.

TEFLON MAN: Jim Corbett fought in the prize ring for 18 years without once receiving so much as a black eye or a bloody nose.

HOOFIN' IT: Paul J. Simpson, of Burlington, North Carolina, ran against a horse in a 144-mile race, and won by 28 miles.

THEY DIDN'T GIVE UP

NEVER SAY DIE: Bobby Walthour, a marathon bicycle racer, was twice pronounced dead during a 60-day race—but he recovered each time and continued to compete.

1/2 FOOT = 63 YARDS: Tom Dempsey, born with only half a right foot, holds the national football record for the longest field goal—63 yards.

DAVID AND GOLIATH: On March 10, 1936, "Pee-Wee" Puett (four feet four inches tall) was the opposing center against "Tiny" Reicher (eight feet one inch tall) in a basketball game between House of David and Tennessee Wesleyan.

ON THE RIGHT TRACK: Wilma Rudolph (above) of Clarksville, Tennessee, won three gold medals for running in the 1960 Olympics, even though she had suffered from polio and worn leg braces as a child.

STRIKING RECOVERY: In 1919, Ray "Slim" Caldwell, a pitcher for the Cleveland Indians, was struck by lightning during a game. He was revived and continued to play.

SCREWBALL SPORTS

WHIFF-LE BALL: Patent #1,664m 367— an exploding golf ball that glows and gives off an odor so it can be easily found—was invented in 1990.

FOWL BALLS: The Poultry Association of Newport, California, uses 16-pound frozen turkeys as bowling balls and one-liter soft-drink bottles as pins.

SEÑOR LANCELOT: Juanito Apinani, a 19th-century matador from Spain, thrilled crowds by using a lance to leap over a charging bull.

THAT'S HITTING THE BOOKS: The first game of table tennis, called "whiff whaff," was played by two students at England's Cambridge University. They used piles of books as a net, champagne corks for balls, and paperbacks as paddles.

TOES AND ARROWS: The Caboclos Indians of Brazil fire their bows most accurately while lying on their backs and bending the bows with their feet.

EXTREME SPORTS

ROLLER MAN: A silvery skinned creature with buglike eyes (left) cruises the streets of Paris after dark. It's Roller Man! Skater Jean-Yves Blondeau dreamed up this futuristic-looking outfit while studying at an industrial design school in Paris. He wears a body suit made of hard latex with 27 wheels attached at knees, back, elbows, hands, and chest, and standard in-line skates. Often going 30 miles per hour, he can morph into 20 perfectly balanced positions. To excel at Jean-Yves's new sport, you need the agility of a hockey player and the balance and flexibility of a gymnast.

CROSSING THE FINN-ISH LINE: Yoga master Wim Hof (right), from Holland, holds the record for ice diving. His record-breaking stunt took place in northern Finland, where two holes, an entrance and an exit, were drilled 164 feet apart. The water was below freezing, just two degrees warmer than the water the *Titanic* passengers froze in. Hof dived through the entrance and began swimming his laps under a two-foot ceiling of ice, following a lighted cord that had been laid on the surface to guide him. One minute, six seconds later, Hof's head sliced through the icy water at the finish line. He had set an ice-diving record.

SKY TENNIS: For Jason Hider (left) and Sally Hathaway, the best tennis court was in the air. One by one they jumped from a plane and, using basic parachuting techniques, adjusted their bodies to get ready to play. Then the game began. Playing tennis while in free fall meant the players had to do a little maneuvering in order to hit the ball. But for these two daredevils, that's what made the game fun.

SENIOR CLASS

ANCIENT GREEK: Age 98 in 1976, Dimitrion Yordanidis from Greece was the oldest person ever to complete a marathon.

TIP-TOP SHAPE: In 1947, Benjamin Fosson, a Swiss mountain guide, climbed Mt. Castor (13,422 feet high) at the age of 88.

BLIND WOMAN'S BLUFF: Margaret Waldron of Jacksonville, Florida, was 74 years old and legally blind when she hit two holes in one on the Amelia Island Plantation Golf Course.

FIT TO BE TEED: Nathaniel Vickers, of Forest Hills, New York, played golf three times a week at the age of 103.

SMALL FRY

LITTLE SLUGGER: In 1952, 12-year-old Joe Reliford, batboy for the professional team the Fitzgerald Pioneers, was sent into the game as a pinch hitter.

HOT SHOT: Frank Wooton, a champion English jockey, won his first race at the age of nine.

LITTLE CLIFF-HANGER: On September 27, 1927, when Lotte Frutiger of Allalinhorn, Switzerland, was only eight years old, she climbed Mount Allalinhorn—which is 13,234 feet high and always covered with ice.

DID YOU KNOW . . .

. . . that baseball umpires in the 1850s wore top hats?

. . . that the National Basketball Association uses 1,150 balls a year? Stacked up, they would reach a height of 910 feet, or about three times the height of the Statue of Liberty.

 . . . that Ty Cobb, who in 1913 earned the highest salary of any outfielder in baseball, was paid $12,000 a year? Compare that to the millions of dollars that players like Derek Jeter (left) and Alex Rodriguez earn today.

. . . that it was common practice in ancient Greece for contestants in the Olympic Games to compete naked?

. . . that John Brallier, the nation's first professional football player, a quarterback for Latrobe, Pennsylvania, in 1895, weighed only 125 pounds?

OVER THE EDGE: Since 1995, fifteen people have been killed in the United States while kayaking. That's why 20-year-old world-class kayaker Tao Berman won't even get into his kayak until he is sure that all the waterfalls along the way are navigable. Berman (below) was the first person to attempt the staggering drop of Johnston Canyon Waterfall at Banff National Park in Alberta, Canada. Equivalent to a jump from a ten-story building, the 98-foot drop is just eight feet wide at the top and lined on both sides with jagged rock. It took Berman less than five seconds to hit the water nose first. A broken paddle and a cut on his shoulder are proof of the kayak's fierce collision with the rocks on the way down. But Berman couldn't have been more elated because he had just taken his kayak where no one had ever gone before.

2
Out of the Odd-inary

The Ripley archives are filled with oddities that reflect Robert Ripley's insatiable curiosity and intense fascination with the bizarre. A peculiar rock formation, a freaky weather phenomenon, an absurd custom, or a grotesque souvenir—as long as it is weird enough, it is sure to find a home in the files of Believe It or Not!

Believe It!

ODD PLACES

MOONBOW: The full moon casts a golden arc across Cumberland Falls in Kentucky. It's the only moonbow in the northern hemisphere.

GOLD GUSH: In Antarctica, an active volcano spews pieces of pure gold when it erupts.

HOLD THE MUSTARD: This hamburger (below) in Cathedral Lakes Provincial Park, British Columbia, is for climbing, not eating.

BEDAZZLED: The snow funnels of the Himalayas are actually huge craters lined with iridescent green ice. The funnels have such a hypnotic effect that travelers feel an urge to leap into the dazzling pits.

DESERT WONDERLAND: An extinct volcano lies in the most arid section of the Sahara desert. Its crater is six miles around and 525 feet deep. The crater contains strange multicolored water surrounded by leafy plants and tall trees, which are home to thousands of birds.

PRETTY IN PINK: Because of its high sulphur content, Red Spring in Saint Nectaire, France, turns anything thrown into its waters to pink stone.

SAND SHOW: In Mexico, mysterious columns of sand appear suddenly and whirl violently—without the slightest breeze.

SPACEY WEATHER

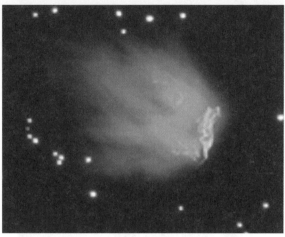

BRANCHING OUT: Arboreal lightning (above), which occurs during tropical storms in South America, looks like the outline of a leafless tree. Unlike normal lightning, its flashes always travel upward.

LOOK OUT BELOW! There are 4,000 man-made satellites flying around in outer space. One striking example is the Hubble Telescope, which at 11.4 tons is roughly the size of a railroad car.

LIGHT SHOW: A meteor shower on November 13, 1833, lit up the sky over North America with 200,000 shooting stars.

SUN CLONES: Five suns rise on misty mornings in Sing-nying-chu, China—but they're only an optical illusion caused by the mist.

ONCE IN A BLUE MOON: In Australia, a tremendous dust storm carrying specks of silica oxide obscured the sun's red and yellow rays, making the moon (right) appear to be blue.

THE SKY IS FALLING! The largest meteorite ever found on Earth fell in 1920 at Hoba West in southwest Africa. It was eight by nine feet and weighed 132,000 pounds. As it streaked through the sky, it probably would have looked even brighter than the meteor pictured above.

LAVA CHASERS: Stephen and Donna O'Meara, who head an organization called Volcano Watch International, have had many close calls. Their research has taught them that a volcano will often erupt most violently soon after it appears to be calmest. The couple had just returned from climbing to the top of a volcano in Costa Rica when it erupted, shooting molten lava into the sky. Within seconds, the very spot they had stood on hours earlier was decimated. The O'Mearas' goal is to be able to predict when a volcano will erupt so that residents will have enough time to evacuate safely.

FLASH: David O. Stillings likes to stalk lightning with a camera. He lives in a part of Florida called Lightning Alley, where there are 90 lightning strikes a year. Carrying the camera increases Stillings's danger, since lightning loves metal.

DEEP FREEZE: While spending six months in Antarctica, Admiral Richard E. Byrd survived temperatures of 83°F below zero in a nine-by-thirteen-foot shack beneath the snow.

POPPING HOT: During the summer of 1947, it was so hot in Missouri that corn popped right off the stalks before it could be harvested.

CURIOUS CUSTOMS

PUP POWER: Nanay children in Siberia travel to and from their distant school on skis pulled by dogs.

LEAF LUGE: Instead of using sleds, Iraku children in Africa slide down mountainsides on large cactus leaves just for fun.

HANDMAID PROTECTION: As a protection against evil, door knockers in Morocco are modeled from the hand of the youngest girl in the household.

TWICE BLESSED: Twins in the Yoruba tribe of Africa command such respect that a mother holding her twins must be given a gift by every passerby she greets.

KNEE-ON LIGHTS: In Israel's Negev Desert, camels are required to wear reflectors on their knees at night.

BALANCING ACT: Women of the Balanta tribe, in Binar, Guinea-Bissau, Africa, annually perform a dance in which they balance on their heads a huge basket containing their husbands or sweethearts.

H$_2$O FOR K9s: A supermarket in Blackhawk, California, sells Thirsty Pup, a bottled water for dogs.

NATURE'S NIGHT-LIGHTS: One of the world's oldest plants grows in Puya Raimondi, in the Cordillera Mountains of Peru. These plants feature blossoms 30 feet high, which are so saturated with resin that shepherds ignite them to light their way.

DEFENSIVE LION: In Belo Horizonte, Brazil, guard lions are used to protect homes from burglars.

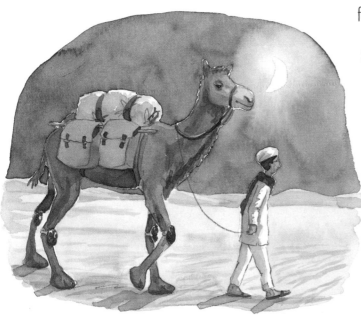

AMAZON.POD: Giant pods that protect the buds on palm trees are used by people of the Brazilian jungle as bathtubs.

NAME-CALLING: It is the custom in Hawaii to give children long, descriptive names when they are born. But with 63 letters, little Kananinoheaokuuhomeo-puukaimanaalohilohinokeaweaweala-makaokalani's name is long even by Hawaiian standards. The boy's sister, shown holding him (above), says his name means *The Beautiful Aroma of My Home at Sparkling Diamond Hill Is Carried to the Eyes of Heaven*—Joe for short.

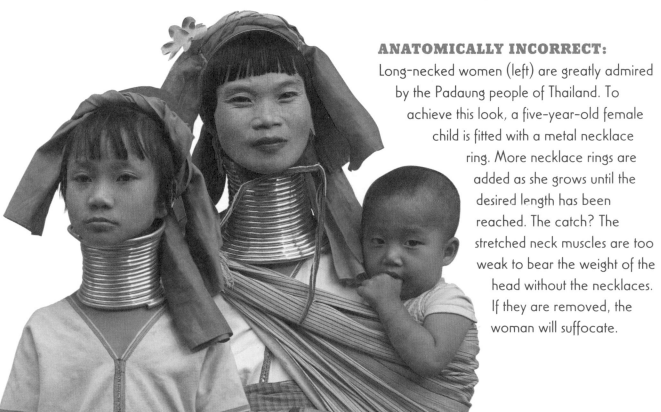

ANATOMICALLY INCORRECT: Long-necked women (left) are greatly admired by the Padaung people of Thailand. To achieve this look, a five-year-old female child is fitted with a metal necklace ring. More necklace rings are added as she grows until the desired length has been reached. The catch? The stretched neck muscles are too weak to bear the weight of the head without the necklaces. If they are removed, the woman will suffocate.

SEA SCRAWLERS: Spines of the sea urchin (right) are used by school children on the Pacific Island of Rarotonga as pencils.

TIBETAN TONGUE-LASHING: The polite way to greet someone in Tibet is to bow and stick out your tongue three times.

EARTH TONES: In Caryville, Florida, there is an annual International Worm Fiddling Contest in which contestants play music to draw earthworms out of the soil.

FEE, FI, FO, FUM: Bean pods in the Union of Myanmar in Asia grow to a height of four feet, and are so sturdy that the Arakanese use them as a stairway to their dwellings.

STICKY SITUATION: Every year, children of Ravensburg, Germany, march through the streets swinging long branches in memory of the 14th-century bubonic plague—a time when people were so afraid of catching the disease, they waved long sticks at one another instead of shaking hands.

CAPTIVATING KEEPSAKES

Here are a few of the more grotesque souvenirs that Ripley brought back from his travels.

THE MASAKICHI STATUE: When a wood-carver (below) found out he was dying, he decided to leave a "living" image of himself to his beloved. After painstakingly plucking the hair from every pore in his body, he inserted each one in corresponding positions on the statue of himself he had carved. He included his eyebrows, and eyelashes, then for the finishing touches, he pulled out his fingernails, toenails, and teeth, and attached them to his sculpture.

FINAL FACIAL: Ancestor skulls (above) from New Guinea were covered with clay.

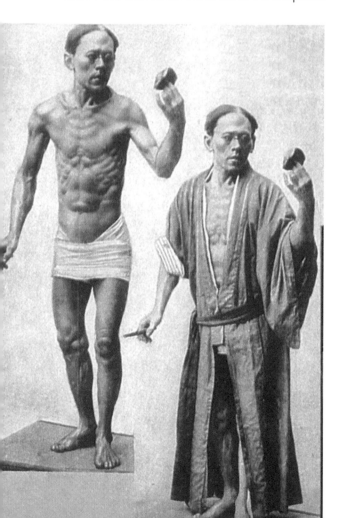

SKULLDUGGERY: A Peruvian Moche Indian skull (right) with parrot feathers, copper eyes, and ponytail, is one of the oldest anthropological exhibits in the Ripley collection. It dates back to A.D. 800.

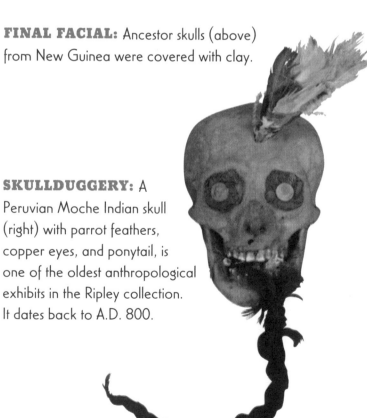

ALL DRESSED UP AND NO PLACE TO GO: Among Ripley's souvenirs is this New Guinea skull and a pig's tooth necklace (right).

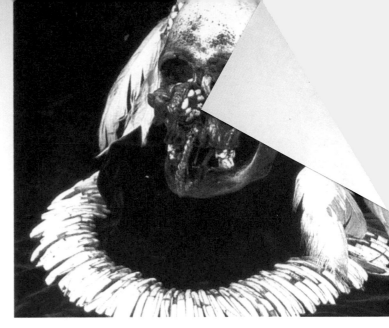

HUMAN RAM-IFICATION: In Tibet, jeweled and silver-plated ram heads (above), used in ceremonial rituals and as decorative objects were fashioned from human skulls.

IRON MAIDEN OF NUREMBERG: Ripley once carried this authentic medieval torture device (right) home from Nuremberg, Germany. Eight feet tall, it is shaped like a coffin and lined with 13 sharp iron spikes, designed to pierce the eyes, throat, and heart of prisoners.

DON'T TRY THIS AT HOME

Legend has it that a red-bearded German scientist, on a quest to discover the secrets of the Jivaro headhunters of the Amazon, disappeared in the rain forest and was never seen alive again. Months later, a trader arrived from Ecuador offering for sale the shrunken head of a man with a red beard.

The practice of head-shrinking has always been a closely guarded tribal secret. No one knows how Robert Ripley obtained this information, but he did. Now the secret, which the unfortunate German scientist lost his life attempting to discover, is about to be revealed to you.

FROM THE PERSONAL FILES OF ROBERT RIPLEY

A Jivaro headhunter began the head-shrinking ritual by cutting off the head of his victim as close to the torso as possible. He then slit the scalp from the crown of the head to the nape of the neck and carefully teased the skull out through this opening. He stretched the skin over a knob of wood and submerged it in boiling water, which made the skin begin to contract.

Next, the Jivaro sewed a ring made of vine into the base of the neck to keep it open during the shrinking process. Hot stones and sand were then dropped inside the head, which the Jivaro kept in constant motion so that the head was heated uniformly. Whenever the sand and stones began to cool, they were emptied out, reheated, and poured back into the head. As the head dried and grew smaller, the Jivaro kneaded and pinched the features constantly to help them retain their lifelike appearance. Finally, the lips were sewn shut. The finished product was about the size of a baseball.

The Jivaros of South America believed that an individual's spiritual powers resided in the head. To decapitate an enemy and possess his head was to keep for one's self all the powers of its original owner. The mouths and other orifices of shrunken heads were often sewn shut to keep the soul from escaping. Ripley kept three fine examples of shrunken heads in his personal collection. He was sure that the hair on the heads grew by several inches while in his possession—proof, he thought, that hair growth continues after death.

A very rare shrunken female head and torso (page 26) is on display in Ripley's Odditiorium in Blackpool, England. Since traditionally the Jivaro did not shrink female heads (shrunken heads are war trophies, and women did not go to war), this artifact was probably deliberately prepared in the early 20th century to sell to tourists.

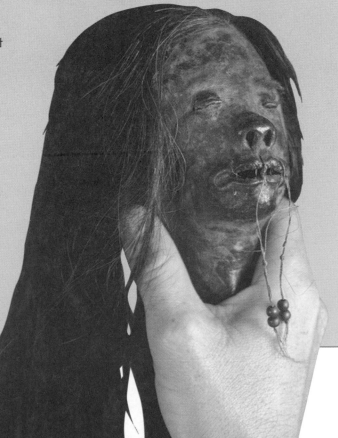

IT'S ABOUT TIME

Owner of one of the world's most unusual collections of clocks and timepieces, Ripley wrote and spoke frequently about the way people kept time all over the world.

HOT FOOT: Medieval monks used a lit candle placed between their toes as an alarm clock. When the flame singed their skin, they knew it was time to rise and shine.

MAN OF THE HOUR: Abu'l Hassan, an Arab poet, invented the hour. He divided the day and night into 24 equal parts in the 13th century.

DON'T FORGET TO DUNK YOUR WATCH: There's a watch that's powered by water, milk, tea, or any type of liquid, but it must be dunked every few days.

DID YOU HEAR ABOUT . . . the alarm clock that can be shut off by shouting at it?

PARALLEL TIME: Have you ever noticed that each pair of horizontally opposing numbers on a clock adds up to twelve?

KING KONG LEFT IT THERE? A giant wristwatch hangs from a 37-story building in Tokyo, Japan.

NO WAY! Fudge, a dog in England, swallowed a musical alarm watch, and until his successful operation, trilled out a tune each morning at 6:45.

3
Humans & Superhumans

No one dared use the word "freak" in the presence of Robert Ripley, who had a deep regard for the unusual people who performed in his Odditoriums, many of whom became his friends. You are about to meet a crowd of men, women, and children from the past and present whose uniqueness will astonish and amaze you.

Believe It!

OUCH!

TONGUE DEPRESSOR: In 1938, Leona Young (above) of Norwich, New York, astounded audiences with her ability to withstand the heat of a plumber's blowtorch on her tongue. Because of this, she was also known as the Devil's Daughter.

PRESSING ENGAGEMENT: Tim Cridland (above), using pain-deadening meditation, lay down on a bed of nails and allowed a 3,000-pound vehicle to drive over him.

A SIGHT FOR SORE EYES: In 1933, Odditorium performer Harry McGreggor (right) used his eyelids to pull a wagon carrying his wife.

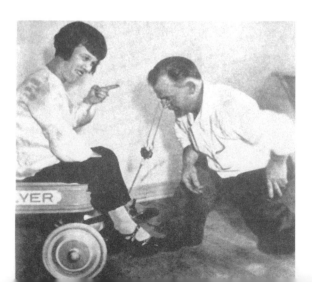

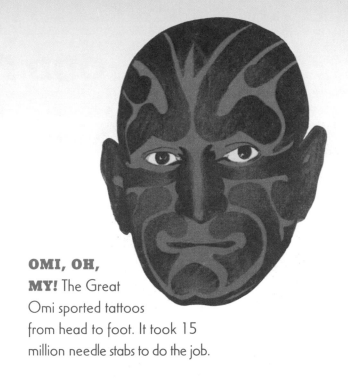

OMI, OH, MY! The Great Omi sported tattoos from head to foot. It took 15 million needle stabs to do the job.

HEAD TRIP: In 1931, entertainer Alexandre Patty (below) climbed up a flight of stairs on his head.

SUSPENSION OF DISBELIEF: Members of the Texas-based Traumatic Stress Discipline Club (above) are hooked on having themselves hoisted into the air by ropes, cables, and pulleys that are attached to multiple hooks pierced through their skin.

SO BEE-COMING: When Fred Wilcutt (left) of Falkville, Alabama, captured a queen bee and placed it under his chin, the hive arranged itself around his jaw and neck like a beard.

ODD FELLOWS

BEFORE

AFTER

QUEEN OF DE-NILE: Elizabeth Christensen (above), 39-year-old wife and mother, believes she is the reincarnation of Queen Nefertiti, who lived 3,000 years ago. Christensen has spent $250,000 on 240 operations to sculpt her face into a likeness of the ancient Egyptian queen.

QUADRUPLE PUPIL: Liu Chung, shown in this wax replica (right), of Shansi, China, was born in A.D. 955 with two pupils in each eye. His unusual anatomy did not deter him from being successful in life—he served as governor of Shansi and minister of state.

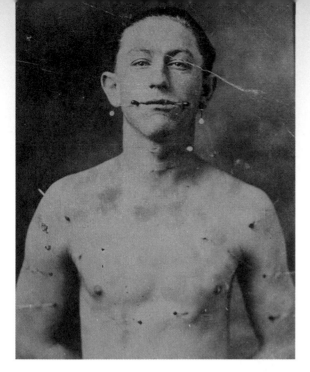

HUMAN PINCUSHION: A. Bryant (left) of Waco, Texas, could stick as many as a hundred pins and needles into his body at the same time.

RUBBER FACE: J.T. Saylors (below) of Memphis, Tennessee, was able to "swallow" his nose.

THE HUMAN UNICORN: This photograph (above) taken in 1928 is of a Manchurian farmer known only as Wang, who had a 13-inch horn on the back of his head.

WHAT A KICK: In the 1930s, Francesco Lentini (left) of Sicily was a master musician and renowned soccer player—an achievement that was no doubt helped by the fact that he was born with three legs.

LEFT OVER AND OVER AGAIN: Every male in the Colombiere family of Nancy, France, was born with two left hands. Perfectly normal in every other way, both their hands had thumbs on the right side.

MESSIE HAIR: French actor Pierre Messie could move his hair at will, causing it to stand, fall, or curl—he could even curl the hair on one side while leaving the other flat.

A BRIGHT IDEA: Ripley met the man shown in this wax replica (right) in Chunking, China, in 1928. Known as Lighthouse Man, he found a way to make the best use of the hole in his head. He simply stuck a seven-inch candle in it and used its light to guide visitors around dark city streets.

 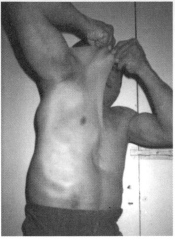

THIN SKIN: While performing, Las Vegas contortionist, Thomas Martin Peres (above), also known as Mr. Stretch, loves to shock people by pulling the skin from his neck over his nose like a turtleneck sweater.

HEAD CASE: This 1937 picture (below) shows Lorraine Chevalier of Philadelphia, Pennsylvania, sitting on her own head. The famous Chevalier family of acrobats claims that only one person is born into their family every 200 years who is capable of attaining this position.

HUMAN OWL: Joe Laurello (above) drew large crowds to Ripley's Odditoriums throughout the 1930s. His ability to swivel his head 180 degrees never failed to amaze them.

BIG, LITTLE, TALL, AND SHORT

THE GENTLE GIANT: Born in 1918, Robert Wadlow (right) of Alton, Illinois, measured eight feet eleven inches and wore a size 37 shoe. In order for him to ride in the family car, the front passenger seat had to be removed to allow room for his long legs. A kind and generous soul, the people of Alton dubbed him "the gentle giant."

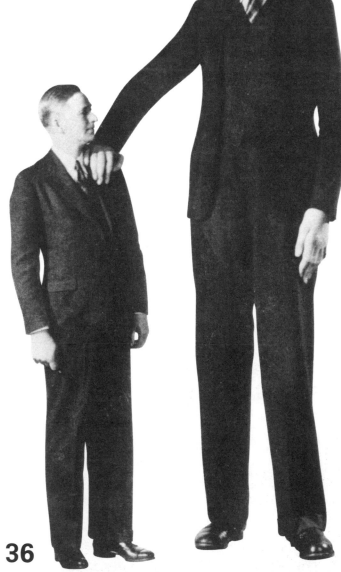

UNDERCOVER: A little person, known only as Richebourg, was a spy just after the French Revolution. Smuggled in and out of France dressed as a baby, he carried messages back and forth in his diapers.

SIX FEET, SEVEN: Igor Ladan of Russia stood six feet tall when he was seven years old.

STIFF COMPETITION: Not everyone can be tall, but there are other ways to get there. Meet the Wolf family. In the mid-1990s, the father held the record for walking on the tallest pair of stilts ever—40 feet 9.5 inches to be exact—that is until his son Travis took the record away from him. Travis hopes he'll keep his title a while longer, but the odds are getting smaller and smaller since siblings Ashley, Tony, and Jordan are well on their way to catching up with him.

BIG FOOT: In 1999, Nike made a size 23 sneaker just for Brad Millard of St. Mary's College in California. This is the largest size sneaker Nike has ever made—even larger than Shaquille O'Neal's, which is a mere size 22. Millard's basketball coach jokes, "When Brad gets a new pair of sneakers, I take the box home and use it as an extra bedroom."

LITTLE BIG MAN: Though he weighed a whopping nine pounds two ounces at birth, Tom Thumb (above) never grew beyond three feet four inches. But that did not keep him from becoming one of the biggest celebrities of his time. Received in the 1860s by the queens of England, France, Spain, and Belgium, his fame helped him amass an immense fortune. In 1863, Tom married Lavinia Warren in a ceremony attended by dignitaries from all over the world. Even President Lincoln sent them a gift. The reception was a lavish affair, featuring an 80-pound wedding cake that weighed more than the bride and groom combined. The tiny couple settled in Connecticut, where they acquired a stable of racehorses, a dazzling yacht, and a mansion filled with antique furniture—miniaturized, of course.

MORE TO LOVE: This baby (above) born in 1936, weighed 92 pounds at the age of six months.

HUMAN COMPUTERS AND BABY BRAINIACS

LARGE HARD DRIVE: Savant Kim Peek, inspiration for the film *Rain Man*, has no separation between the left and right side of his brain, which is one-third larger than normal. Because his brain has no filtering mechanism, it saves every piece of information it receives. Perhaps this explains why Peek was able to memorize his first book when he was 16 months old and why he cannot only tell you the day of the week for any date in history, but also every word of the more than 8,000 books he's read so far.

MOST NOTEWORTHY: Mozart (below) could write down, note for note, symphonies he had heard just once.

BABY TAPE RECORDER: Murasaki Shikibu possessed such a remarkable memory that, at the age of two, she was able to repeat 1,000 lines of poetry after hearing them only once.

NO PROBLEM: At the age of four, Kim Ung-Young of Seoul, South Korea, could solve math problems based on Einstein's theory of relativity.

FULLY COMMITTED: Elija, The Gaon, chief rabbi of Lithuania, never forgot a book— he committed 2,500 volumes, including the Bible and Talmud, to memory, and could repeat any passage from them at will.

GRAVELY UNSETTLING: Nicholas Settle of New York could walk through any cemetery and recite the epitaphs on each tombstones from memory.

BIG AND LITTLE POWERHOUSES

GIRL POWER: Shannon Pole Summer (above) is only 14 years old, but she can pull a truck packed with members of her school's football team—a combined weight of 12,720 pounds.

SUPPORTIVE HUSBAND: In the late 1890s, Louis Cyr, famous Canadian strongman, supported his 125-pound wife as she climbed a ladder that he held in one outstretched hand.

HUMAN BRIDGE: Eighteenth-century strongman Thomas Topham of Derby, England, could lie between two chairs with four men standing on his body while he lifted a six-foot table with his teeth.

NICE KITTY: German circus performer Miss Heliot entertained audiences in 1953 by carrying a 660-pound lion on her shoulders.

STRONG-ARM TACTIC: Allen Durwood, bodyguard to King Malcolm McAnmore of Scotland, was able to keep 20 assassins from entering the castle by holding the door closed with just his arm.

ALL ABOUT YOU— BELIEVE IT OR NOT!

Your brain, with its ten billion nerve cells, can record over 86 million pieces of information every day, and your memory can hold 100 trillion facts during your lifetime.

- There are over 9,000 taste buds in your tongue.

- By the time you reach 70, you will have shed 40 pounds of skin.

- There are 625 sweat glands in each square inch of your skin.

- Your body contains enough potassium to fire a small cannon and enough carbon to fill 900 pencils.

- A mouse has more bones than you do. The little critter has 225 bones. You have just 206.

- It takes more energy to frown than to smile. You only need 17 muscles to create a smile, but a frown requires 43.

- If all the blood vessels in your body were placed end to end, they would stretch 12,000 miles.

- The lenses in your eyes will continue to grow throughout your lifetime.

UPLIFTING PERFORMANCE: German strongwoman Katherine Wermke was 17 when she lifted a piano and its player.

TINY CHAIRMAN: At the age of five months, Victor Casados, Jr., could lift two chairs weighing nine pounds each at the same time.

WELL-BALANCED: In 1953, 148-pound Bob Dotzauer (below) balanced three lawnmowers on his chin—which, combined, weighed five pounds more than he did.

WEIRD MEDICINE

Enlarged photo of bullet

Mr. W.V. Meadows

SLUGGISH RECOVERY: W.V. Meadows (above) of West Point, Georgia, was shot in the eye at the Battle of Vicksburg on July 1, 1863. Fifty-eight years later he unexpectedly coughed up the Civil War slug.

CANINE CANCER DETECTOR: With a higher success rate than an X-ray, a former bomb-sniffing dog by the name of George has been retrained to sniff out cancer in people.

TOO MUCH INFORMATION?
A company in Tokyo, Japan, sells The Breath Alert and Fit Scan, a device that records how bad your breath is, and measures your body fat.

SCROLLWORK: Physicians in ancient Egypt were accompanied on house calls by an aide who read directions for each treatment from a scroll.

TUMMY TUCK: Alfred Hitchcock, the famous film director, did not have a belly button. He had it surgically removed.

CHAIRSIDE MANNER: Purpose 1, an egg-shaped robotic armchair, is programmed to give psychiatric counseling—from Freudian psychology to meditation to music therapy.

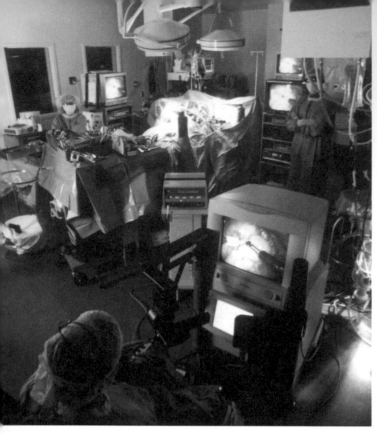

REMOTE-CONTROL SURGERY:

Though closed-chest heart surgery (left) was developed by NASA for operating on astronauts in space, surgeon Dr. Douglas Boyd found the perfect test subject here on Earth. Farmer John Penner, who had suffered a heart attack, could not be away from his work for the three months he'd need to recover from conventional heart surgery. That's why he agreed to try remote-control surgery. The procedure took place on October 6, 1999, in an operating room that looked like the site of a virtual-reality game. Holes less than one-fourth inch wide were made in Penner's chest so three robotic arms could fit inside and perform the surgery. Dr. Boyd, sitting six feet away from his patient, guided the arms by remote control. The operation was a success, and the recovery period was so drastically reduced that Penner was back tending his cows in three days.

GOLDEN OPPORTUNITY: In the late 1800s, Dr. O.H. Simpson, a dentist in Dodge City, Kansas, prepared the gold he needed for filling teeth by placing twenty dollar gold pieces on the Santa Fe Railroad tracks so that passing trains would flatten them. It's a good thing he didn't flatten himself!

MAGGOT MEDICINE: When antibiotics and a scalpel were unable to save diabetic Tom Hancock's foot, fly larvae, nature's tiniest microsurgeons, came to the rescue. When it comes to curing infections, maggots are used today as a last resort when conventional treatments have failed, and amputation is the only other alternative. The maggots, bred in a special lab, clean wounds by eating dead tissue and harmful bacteria. There's only one catch—they have to be removed within 72 hours or they'll turn into flies!

BEE-STING THERAPY: Multiple sclerosis patient Pat Wagner has obtained outstanding relief from stiffness and pain by allowing dozens of bees to sting her each day. The medical community is not sure why this is an effective treatment for the symptoms of this debilitating disease.

HAIR-RAISING EXPERIENCE:
In Trier, Germany, bald people who wanted to grow hair paid farmers to have their heads licked by cows.

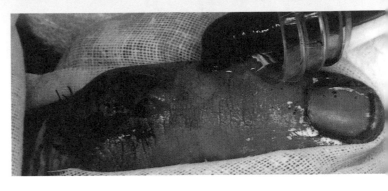

BLOODSUCKERS: This finger (above) was cut off in an accident. But thanks to leech therapy, a natural way of healing, it was possible for the finger to be reattached to its owner's hand. Leech therapy was also used successfully on Justin Page, a little boy whose ear was nearly severed by a dog bite. He needed microsurgery to reconnect his ear, but the veins were too badly damaged. Since there was nowhere for the excess blood to flow, it pooled around the injury, making it impossible for healing to take place. So medicinal leeches were attached to the area to drain it. A leech can take in five times its body weight in 20 minutes. The process doesn't hurt because a leech's saliva contains painkillers.

43

DID YOU HEAR ABOUT . . .

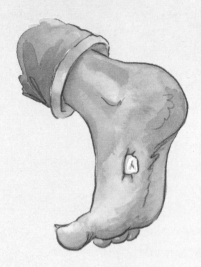

. . . the boy who went to the doctor for his sore foot—only to find that a tooth was growing in his instep?

. . . the world's first drive-through vaccination clinic that opened in Pomona, California, in 1990?

. . . the man who came out of the hospital after recovering from a stroke and then suddenly began speaking with a Scandinavian accent?

. . . the surgeon named Dr. William Gorgas, who operated on a soldier by the light from a jar of fireflies?

. . . the medicine made from mouse ashes mixed with honey that was used as a remedy for earaches in ancient Rome?

DID YOU KNOW . . .

. . . that Komodo dragon saliva (above) may hold the key to surviving biological warfare? These lizards are immune to one another's poisonous saliva. Researcher Terry Fredeking is studying the venom to discover the secret of its disease-preventing properties.

. . . that the eye of the Egyptian god Horus was an ancient symbol of protection and healing, and is the source of the sign Rx, used by modern physicians on prescriptions?

4
Everywhere & All the Time

When asked, "Where do you get all your facts?" Ripley always replied, "Everywhere and all the time." Our universe is full of more incredible things than we can possibly imagine. The following is an assortment of mind-boggling facts from the past and present files of Believe It or Not!

Believe It!

HOW DO THEY DO IT?

SOMETIMES YOU FEEL LIKE A NUT: Some natives of the South Pacific (left) can walk up the highest coconut trees without using rope or gear of any kind.

DOUBLE CROSS: The Adung River Bridge in Tibet consists only of a rope 150 feet long strung 40 feet above the water. To get from one side to the other, women with babies strapped to their backs hang upside down in a ring made from reeds and pull themselves across.

RESPECT YOUR ELDERS: On December 10, 1997, Julia "Butterfly" Hill (right) climbed 180 feet up an ancient redwood tree in a bold attempt to save a forest from being cut down. She did not come down for two years. Enclosed in a dome of multicolored tarps, Hill lived on a tiny wooden platform, using a bucket for a toilet, candles for light, and a one-burner propane stove to cook on. A ground crew brought her supplies, which she pulled up with ropes. During her record-breaking time in the tree, Hill endured 90-mile-per-hour winds and harassment by lumber company helicopters. She came down only when the company agreed to protect the surrounding three acres from logging.

AMAZING FEET: On August 6, 1938, people gasped in astonishment as they watched Kuda Bux (below) of India walk through fire. A 20-inch ditch outside of Radio City Music Hall in New York had been filled with a layer of fiery coals. Twenty-four hours later, the temperature inside the pit had reached 1,400°F. After walking barefoot up to his ankles through the hot coals, Kuda Bux was examined by doctors who found no injuries.

HIGH ON THEMSELVES: In Belgium, a group of men called *Les Echassiers* (above), perform combat moves, kicking and hopping while on stilts. The tradition dates back to the 15th century.

SUSPENDED ANIMATION: In 1837, to demonstrate the power of meditation, a yogi named Haridas allowed himself to be buried alive for 40 days. In preparation for the ordeal, the mystic went into a self-induced trance. Before burying him, his assistants filled his ears, nose, and mouth with wax, and wrapped him in a blanket. A guard was posted at his "grave" to make sure that no trickery took place. When the assistants dug Haridas up, he was extremely thin, but otherwise in perfect shape.

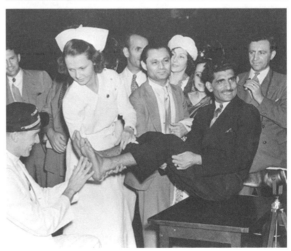

WHY DO THEY DO IT?

JUNK FOOD: Michel Lotito, long considered a medical mystery, found that his unusual ability to chew and swallow indigestible household objects such as razor blades, nuts, bolts, china, glasses, and cutlery could be parlayed into a career. To date he has ingested a grocery cart, a bicycle, a coffin, and a complete Cessna airplane.

RIVETING PERFORMANCE: Bill Steed, a professor of frog psychology at Croaker College in the 1980s, used hypnosis to train frogs to perform amazing feats such as lifting barbells (below).

THE WRITE STUFF: In 1942, Lena Deeter (below) of Conway, Arkansas, amazed audiences by showing them how she could simultaneously write with both hands in different directions.

ON PINS AND NEEDLES: A popular amusement among the rural population of Bohemia is the annual pin-sticking contest to determine the best human pincushion. In 1928, the king of the local gypsy tribe won the contest by enduring 3,200 needles in his arm for a period of 31 hours. His record has never been broken.

SKETCHY STUNT: In 1936, a Dallas Odditorium performer drew three different cartoons simultaneously using both hands and a foot.

YOU'VE GOT TO BE KIDDING!

NO SNAKES IN THE GRASS: Women snake worshippers of Dahomey, Africa, are obliged to pick up every snake they encounter and transport it to the nearest temple—wound around their necks like necklaces!

BEASTLY WELCOME: Writer and naturalist Charles Watertown slept with a slow, shaggy, tree-dwelling mammal called a sloth, and frequently greeted his guests while growling and crawling on all fours.

HI-TECH HOWARD: In 1938, millionaire Howard Hughes (above) set a round-the-world speed record, flying at 352.39 miles per hour in a plane that was filled with Ping-Pong balls. He brought them all so they would cushion his fall and keep him afloat in case he crashed into the ocean.

MULE'S GOLD: A donkey named Ichimonji, once a resident of the Tokyo Zoo, was fitted with a complete set of gold-filled dentures.

FOWL FASHION: During the 1700s, Ignatz von Roll, a turkey farmer in Germany, had all of his birds fitted with tiny Turkish turbans.

HE'S GOT MAIL

From the beginning, Ripley welcomed letters from fans, who gave him some of his best ideas. After he began running contests for the best Believe It or Nots, he began to get 90% of his material for free. During the 1930s and '40s, Ripley received more than a million letters per year. That's 3,500 letters per day. "All the world does my work," chortled Ripley, "and I don't have to pay 'em a cent!"

BANANAGRAM: On July 19, 1988, Rachela Colonna received this properly addressed, stamped banana through the mail. It was sent by her niece to St. Raphael's Hospital where Colonna was a patient. On one side was the address, and on the other were the words "I love you" in Italian.

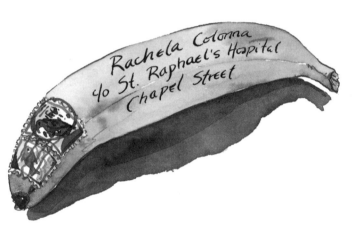

Rachela Colonna
¼ St. Raphael's Hospital
Chapel Street

KIDDY EXPRESS: In 1858, Tom Caldwell became the regular U.S. mail carrier between Fort Scott and Osage Mission, Kansas, riding 40 miles on horseback each trip—and he was only 12 years old.

CANINE DELIVERY: For a three-year period in the late 1800s, a German shepherd dog named Dorsey was the only mail carrier between Calico and Bismarck in California's Mojave Desert. He never once missed his regular schedule on the three-mile trip.

MAIL MINUTIA: Tom Higgins of San Diego, California, who first started writing to Ripley in the 1940s, had nearly 500 of his submissions turned into Believe It or Not! cartoons over a period of 60 years—more than any other single individual.

SLIM PICKIN'S: The first phone book was published in New Haven, Connecticut, in 1878 and contained only 50 names and addresses.

PUTTING A GOOD FACE ON IT: Canadians can send letters with personalized postage stamps that display their own photos.

BRANCH OFFICE: For 25 years, the post office of Appleton, England, was an ancient oak tree with a hollow trunk— 40 feet in circumference.

PENNY-WISE: General Zachary Taylor almost lost the nomination for president of the United States when the letter asking him to accept the honor was returned unopened by Taylor because it was sent "postage collect."

LOGGING ON, SOUTHERN STYLE: In La Grange, Georgia, nearly all of the 27,000 residents receive free Internet service courtesy of the city.

HUMPBACK DELIVERY: In the 1960s, mail was carried over the Dead Heart desert in Australia in an engineless automobile pulled by camels.

PHENOMENAL FASHION

FROM HEAD . . .

SHIPSHAPE: Three feet tall, this headdress was worn by Marie Antoinette, who married King Louis XVI and reigned as queen of France from 1771 to 1792.

KNEE-JERK FASHION: In 16th-century Germany, before the invention of the wristwatch, fashionable young men strapped hourglasses to their knees to help them tell time.

. . . TO TOE

FOOTNOTES: Musicians of ancient Greece wore shoes that played music when they walked.

FOOTLOOSE: Shoes in Colonial America could be worn on either foot.

IT'S THE BUZZ! In ancient Greece, women wore live cicadas leashed to golden thread as ornaments for their hair.

WHAT GOES AROUND COMES AROUND: Open-toed shoes were the height of fashion in the year A.D. 615.

SUIT SOWER: One day the seed of an idea for a new act popped into performance artist Gene Pool's (pictured above with a friend) head. Why not grow a suit out of grass and then get chased by a lawn mower? He did just that and, in the process, discovered that he had a green thumb. Not one to let the grass grow under his feet, Pool started his own clothing line and has perfected his art to the point where he can now grow an entire three-piece suit in just two weeks. Grass cars are another of his specialties.

ALL THE NEWS THAT'S FIT TO WEAR: It took Mrs. Willis N. Ward and Mrs. John Hoppemath (above) the better part of 1939 to make these newsprint coats.

SUITED TO YOUR MOOD: A heat-sensitive bathing suit was invented by Donald Spector of Union City, New Jersey. Made of material that is thermally sensitive, it changes color as its wearer's body temperature fluctuates according to mood.

ALL BUTTONED DOWN: Owen Totten (right) of Mt. Erie, Illinois, is quite attached to his button suit, made with 5,600 buttons, no two of which are alike.

ROYAL ODDBALLS

STIRRING TRIBUTE: To honor King John III of Poland's victory in war, the original bagel was baked in the shape of the circular stirrups used by the Polish cavalry in 1683.

HAD THEIR CAKE AND HEARD IT, TOO! In 1533, a huge cake served at the wedding of the Duke of Orleans (who became King Henry II of France) and Catherine de Médicis contained, within its edible contents, a four-piece orchestra.

HOW FESTIVE: When fried, the white of a murre's egg turns bright blue, while the yolk turns red.

SEE-FOOD DIET: Emperor Charles V of Germany ate at least 60 distinct courses every day of his life.

NEW TWIST: Pretzels were invented in southern France in A.D. 610 by French monks, who shaped them to look like a child's arms folded in prayer.

GEM OF A MEAL: King Henry III of France dined regularly on partridges coated with solid gold, omelets sprinkled with ground-up pearls, and poultry soaked in expensive perfume.

WHEN IN ROME: The most popular dessert at ancient Roman banquets was a sweet onion.

ROYAL SHOCK ABSORBERS: In Germany, during the 19th century, all princes had a *purgelknaben*: a boy who was brought up with the young prince and was spanked every time the prince misbehaved.

PUPPY LOVE: King Henry III of France, who ruled from 1574 to 1589, was so fond of pets that whenever his favorite dog had a litter, he would carry the puppies for days in a basket slung around his neck.

LOVEBIRDS: To appease the gods, Khanderav, ruler of Baroda, India, from 1856 to 1870, spent $200,000 to host 42 marriage ceremonies. In each case, the bride and groom were pigeons.

A DOG'S LIFE: The eighth Earl of Bridgewater, who died in 1829, dressed his dogs in fine clothing and allowed them to have dinner at his table every day.

BATH LORE

Bath Ban: Caligula (A.D.12–41), while emperor of Rome, made taking a bath a crime punishable by death.

Clean Getaway: At a hotel on Honshu, Japan's Wakayama Peninsula, guests can take baths in a cable car as it crosses a deep gorge.

Dirty Trick: In the 1930s in Howe, Indiana, a woman, known locally as the Animal Woman, lived with skunks and did not bathe or change her clothes for 25 years. As if to prove the wisdom of her lifestyle, she died ten days after she was given a bath.

Bath Phobia: Queen Isabela of Spain (1451–1504) was proud of the fact that she had taken but two baths in her life— once when she was born and the other when she was married.

Tubby Commander in Chief: William Howard Taft, president of the United States from 1909 to 1913, was so huge that he needed an extra-large bathtub. In fact, four workmen once sat in it comfortably.

YUCKY AND GROSS

HEDGEHOG HONOR ROLLS: Schoolboys in Morocco are fed the roasted livers of hedgehogs to help improve their studies.

ABORIGINAL ORIGINAL: Moth larvae, anyone? For the Australian Aborigines, they're a favorite snack.

BUG-PLATTER SPECIAL: Pork-stuffed cricket is a favorite in Myanmar, southeast Asia.

JUICY JEWELRY: In New Guinea, sago-maggots are worn as jewelry, but can also serve as an instant snack for hungry travelers.

CRISPY CRITTERS: In Oaxaca, Mexico, grasshoppers fried in garlic and lemon are a favorite snack.

DYE-ING OF THIRST: Pink lemonade was invented when a circus performer unwittingly used a bucket of water to make lemonade in which another performer had soaked his red tights.

TRICK OR TREAT? New Guinea isn't the only place where you can munch on creepy-crawlies. A lucky few in the United States have discovered a company that makes lollipops embedded with worms, and an amber-colored candy called InsectNside, filled with real bugs. *Bon appétit!*

FOOD ODDITIES

ANTIQUE OMELET: Chinese eggs that are sold as delicacies in Singapore are often 100 years old.

HOTHOUSE ICE CREAM: Orchid ice cream in Turkey is made from the dried tubers of wild orchids.

FOOD FOR THOUGHT: Josie Holton published 100 copies of all 625 verses of Samuel Taylor Coleridge's *The Rime of the Ancient Mariner* printed on edible seaweed.

GOT SHEETS? Milk is sold in sheets in Denmark—to drink it, add hot water and refrigerate.

56

5

Critters

The Ripley files are chock-full of unbelievable
facts about the animals who share our world.
Here are some you may not know.

Believe It!

CREATURE FEATURES

LEAVES ALONE: The koala bear (left) of Australia rarely takes a drink. Except in times of drought, it gets all the fluid it needs from the eucalyptus leaves it eats. In the Aborigine language, *koala* means "no drink."

DON'T MAKE A PEEP! Some goats have a strange survival technique. When the goats are startled or surprised, their muscles lock and they fall over, literally paralyzed with fear, until they feel safe again.

SAWTOOTH: A beaver can chomp down a tree five inches in diameter in three minutes.

SWEATING BLOOD: A hippopotamus has sweat that looks like blood, but it's really a kind of skin conditioner.

PETITE FEET: The klipspringer antelope (above) of Africa has such small feet that all four of its hooves can fit on a dime.

POCKET-SIZED: Only one-inch long, a newborn kangaroo could hide behind a postage stamp.

KISS AND TELL: Prairie dogs (below) identify each other by kissing.

RUFFLED FEATHERS: The hummingbird (above) is the only bird that can fly backward. All it has to do is reverse the direction of its feathers.

BIG MOUTH: The blue whale has a mouth so large that a human can stand inside it, yet it swallows nothing larger than a shrimp.

HOW CLEVER

FRESH STEPS: A fawn (above), one of the most helpless of newborn creatures, has built-in protection—it leaves no scent.

EYE CONTACT: The red-capped mangabeys (below) of Africa talk to one another by blinking their white eyelids in a secret Morse-like code only they can understand.

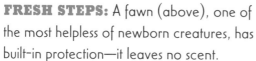

FEATHERED GENIUS: When Irene Pepperberg (above), a professor at the University of Arizona, says good night, she typically hears the reply, "Bye. I'm gonna go eat dinner. I'll see you tomorrow." Though the response itself is not unusual, the source is. It comes from Alex, an African gray parrot, Pepperberg's main research subject for the past 22 years. Since working with Pepperberg, Alex has developed a 100-word vocabulary and can identify 50 different objects and sort them by color, shape, and texture. What Pepperberg's study has proven is that Alex is not merely "parroting" what he hears but actually processing information.

BODY LANGUAGE: Elephants send messages over long and short distances by a "secret language" of low-frequency sounds, believed to be caused by a fluttering spot on their foreheads.

HUGE TALENT: When Suti, a 6,500-pound African elephant, lived at Chicago's Lincoln Park Zoo, he painted abstract works of art.

THE BETTER TO SCARE YOU: The rifle bird of Australia decorates its nest with a snake's skin to frighten away predators.

A MINI WEBSITE: The hummingbird makes its nest out of spiderwebs.

INTERIOR DECORATORS: Male satin bowerbirds actually paint the walls of their nest with a fiber brush dipped in charcoal and berry juice. They accessorize it with flowers, shells, and shiny stones to enhance the overall effect.

TAKE A BOW: An elephant is the only animal with four knees.

SNEAK ATTACK: The California roadrunner can capture a rattlesnake by piling sharp cactus spines around the snake while it's sleeping.

BLOODTHIRSTY: The vampire bat (below) drinks more than its own weight in blood every night.

CURIOUS COMPANIONS

THE FOX AND THE HOUND: A fox and a foxhound, both owned by the Belstone Hunt in England, became the best of friends.

GORILLA GRIEF: Koko, a gorilla who understands the meaning of at least 500 words in sign language, cried for two days when she was told of the death of her pet cat.

PURR-FECT FOSTER MOM: A cat owned by A.W. Mitchell of Vancouver, British Columbia, nurtured 25 baby chicks (above).

CANINE CAT-SCANNER: Ginny, a dog owned by Philip Gonzalez, seeks out and rescues stray cats from Dumpsters, air conditioning ducts, and other dangerous places. Sometimes she rescues as many as eight injured cats in a week. There's even a charity named after her, the Ginny Fund, that provides money to help cats find good homes and to help pay their veterinary bills.

FIN POWER: This waterskiing chimp (right) is being towed by a dolphin!

GUARD GOOSE: A Canada goose on a farm near Yakima, Washington, has bonded with a Siberian husky. It sleeps in the doghouse, shares the dog's food, and fights other dogs that try to enter their doghouse.

SNOOZE ALARM: Novelist Charles Dickens (1812–1870), who wrote many fine classics, including *A Christmas Carol* and *Oliver Twist*, had a deaf cat that reminded him when it was bedtime by snuffing out the candle on his desk.

RULING THE ROOSTER: O.J. Plomesen of Luverne, Minnesota, owned this rooster named Golden Duke (below), who could actually pull a carriage containing Plomesen's baby daughter down Main Street.

HITCHING A RIDE: This dog and cat (below) clearly don't know they're not supposed to like each other.

63

HOW THOUGHTFUL!

HAIR-LINED NEST: The white-eared honeyeater is a timid bird. Yet it steals the hair off passersby to line its nest and make it soft for its babies.

THANKS FOR SHARING: All a baby herring gull has to do to get its lunch is peck the red spot on its mother's beak, and she'll throw up the fish she just ate to feed it.

WATCH BIRD: By chattering loudly and incessantly, the toppie, an African bird, never fails to warn passersby of the presence of a hidden snake.

SPECIAL DELIVERY: Male Siberian djungarian hamsters act as midwives to their mates, helping them to give birth, then opening the babies' airways and licking them clean.

SEEING EYE HORSE: A miniature horse named Twinky (below) has been trained as a guide animal for the blind. A horse has a life span four times that of a dog, a 350-degree field of vision, and an inexpensive diet—the bale of hay it eats per month costs just four dollars. Twinky tends to slip and slide at the mall, so he has been fitted with little sneakers to improve his traction.

TECHNO-RAT: Dr. Judy Reevis, an information technologist, wanted to hook up an old classroom to the Internet. The cramped space above the ceiling made it impossible for her to do the wiring herself, so she decided to train a rat to do the work. First she tied a string around a rat she calls Ratty and attached the other end to a line of cable. She then sent Ratty, who can pull up to 250 feet of cable at a time, through the ceiling to do his job. Dr. Reevis knocked on the ceiling to keep him moving in the right direction. To date, Ratty has wired ten schools.

MY DOG DID MY HOMEWORK:
Isaac, the calculating canine, is a five-year-old golden retriever that can add, subtract, multiply, divide, and even do square roots. When Isaac was a puppy, his owner, Gary Wimer, began spending 20 minutes a day teaching him to count. The puppy loved his lessons and soon began astounding everyone who came into contact with him. All Wimer has to do is ask the little genius what the square root of 36 is, and Isaac will bark six times. He even helps Wimer's six-year-old with his arithmetic. Now that's a dog you can count on.

TOP DOG: Endal, a Labrador retriever (below), was named Dog of the Millennium by a dog food company for his super-canine efforts to help his owner, Allen Parton. Parton suffers from memory loss and partial paralysis sustained while serving in the Royal Navy during the Gulf War. With the help of Endal's trainers at Canine Partners for Independence in Hampshire, England, he and Endal have developed a special sign language. When Parton forgets the names of things, all he has to do is tap the top of his head, touch his cheek, or rub his hands together, and Endal will fetch his hat, his razor, or his gloves. The dog can also pick up items from supermarket shelves, withdraw money from the ATM, and load and unload the washer and dryer.

NICE SAVES

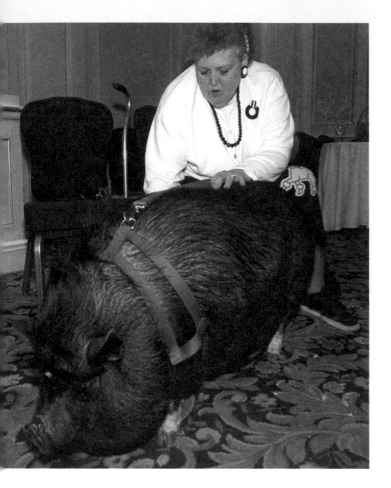

THIS LITTLE PIGGY PLAYED DEAD:
In Beaver Falls, Pennsylvania, residents treat a potbelly pig named Lulu (left) like royalty. That's because she literally saved the life of her owner. Jo Altsaman was home alone the morning she suffered a massive heart attack. When she fell to the floor, Lulu lay her head on Altsaman's chest and cried real tears. Then she sprang into action and went for help. First she squeezed her body through the doggie door that was only one foot wide. Then she ran into the road where she lay down and played dead to get someone's attention. Minutes later, a young man stopped. Lulu got up and led the man to the trailer. When he knocked on the door, Altsaman answered faintly, "Call 911." At the hospital, doctors credited Lulu with saving Altsaman's life.

PORPOISE WITH A PURPOSE: For a period of 20 years, from 1790 to 1810, a white porpoise named Hatteras Jack guided every ship in and out of Hatteras Inlet, off the coast of North Carolina, and never lost a single vessel.

EARLY WARNING SYSTEMS: Many animals can detect sounds and movements that cannot be perceived by humans. Before the Chilean city of Talcuhuana was struck by an earthquake in 1835, all the dogs had deserted the town. And before a quake hit the French Riviera in 1887, horses all over the area refused to eat and tried to break out of their stalls. Even the birds in the trees fluttered about in a frenzy.

THERE'S NO PLACE LIKE HOME

GOOD MEWS: Fluffy, a kitten owned by Mrs. Clyde McMillan, appeared at the newspaper that had published a want ad asking for its return.

BETTER LATE THAN NEVER: Clem, a cat, returned to his owner, Kurt Helminiak of Bancroft, Wisconsin, after an eight-year absence.

I'M BACK! Trixie, a collie lost from John Eaton's car in Oklahoma, appeared a month later at her owner's home in Phoenix, Arizona, a distance of 1,000 miles.

IT'S A GOOD THING I'M SO SMART: Bobby, a parakeet lost for 18 hours in Withywood, England, was returned to its owner after announcing its name and address.

DID YOU MISS ME? Popcorn, a cat owned by Nancy Beecham, disappeared when her family moved from Oahu, Hawaii, to La Mesa, California. The cat was found seven weeks later in a cat carrier, elated to see her owners after having gone 49 days without food.

EXTRA PARTS

Once in a while, nature produces an animal with too many—or too few—parts. These unusual creatures fascinated Robert Ripley, who filled his Odditoriums with as many as he could.

TWO TAILS
The better to scare with!

TWO HEADS
The better to think with!

SIX LEGS
The better to leap with!

TWO NOSES
The better to smell with!

MISSING PARTS

Short on legs, long on attitude: This pup could run almost as fast as its four-legged friends, even though it had no hips or hind legs.

Gets more attention this way: Barney Lederman showed off his beakless chicken in a Chicago bar.

Gets by with a little help from his friends: Born without front legs, this pony needed support to walk upright.

Ichabod Chicken: A chicken in Elizabethtown, Kentucky, laid an egg—which wouldn't be so remarkable if the chicken wasn't missing its head.

UNDER THE SEA

FISH WHO FISH: The angler fish of Panama attracts its food by the light on the end of its nose.

DON'T MESS WITH ME: The boxfish is so ferocious that if swallowed by a shark, it can bite its way to freedom.

FISH WHO HUNT: The African catfish leaves the water at night to hunt on land.

THE BETTER TO EAT YOU: The wolf fish (below) has such a vicious bite that its teeth will leave marks on an iron anchor.

FISH WHO SHOOT: The rifle fish of Asia spits water at its prey with such force that the prey is knocked to the surface where the rifle fish can easily gulp it down. This miniature marksman is able to hit targets 50 feet away.

SLIPPERY PARTNERS: Lamprey eels work in pairs to carry heavy stones along the bottom of the sea. They use them to construct nests that can be three feet high and four feet around.

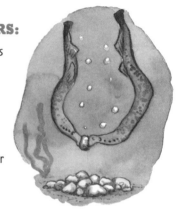

MINI ME: When it raises its dorsal fin, the scorpion fish has a built-in decoy that looks like a small fish, complete with imitation eye and mouth. Attracted by the lure, the scorpion fish's prey swims closer to get a better look—and in the blink of an eye becomes a tasty dinner for the scorpion fish.

HOW CONVENIENT: If a lobster loses an eye, it just grows another. And in a ten-year period, the tiger shark produces and sheds over 24,000 teeth.

FALLS APART: When frightened, the starfish snaps off all its arms.

MAKES ITSELF SICK: The sea cucumber defends itself by throwing up its own digestive system in order to entangle and trap its attacker.

WEARS SQUISHY ARMOR: To make itself unappealing to predators, the sea sponge crab cuts a piece of sponge that it then fits perfectly over its back.

THEY STICK TOGETHER: Baby eels travel in such tight formations that they often look like a ball of yarn.

THE BETTER TO FIND YOU: Giant squid have eyes the size of basketballs.

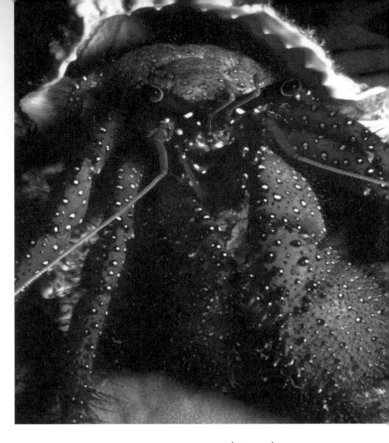

LIVE-IN HELP: The hermit crab (above) lives in the abandoned shells of other creatures with a sea worm that keeps the place clean.

FISH TALES

WHAT A SPECTACLE: When caught, this fish (left) was wearing the glasses of a fisherman who had lost them not long before.

TWO BOATS ARE BETTER THAN ONE: Women of Palimbai, New Guinea, fish by holding a huge net between them while precariously balancing in the prows of two small canoes.

GLOW FOR IT: Canadian Paul Giannaris has invented a chemical formula that causes worms to glow in the dark, making them the perfect bait for fishing.

SMALL LAKE, BIG NAME: Charoggagoggmanchaugagoggchaubunagungamaug, the local Native American name for a lake in Massachusetts, means "You fish on your side, I fish on my side, nobody fishes in the middle."

FEEDING FRENZY: A pike swallowed a bass that had swallowed a perch that had swallowed a minnow that was on a hook, that was on a line held by E.F. Bush of Detroit, Michigan.

NOSY FISH: Harry Morse, age six, caught a six-pound trout in Lake Keuka, New York, when the fish leaped into his boat and clamped its jaws on the young man's nose.

BEARLY MADE IT: While fishing in Lake Timagami, Canada, Dr. I.H. Alexander of Pittsburgh, Pennsylvania, was suddenly startled by a bear that climbed into his rowboat. Since Dr. Alexander couldn't swim, he rowed the boat and bear to shore.

UNTANGLED WEB: When New Guinea fishermen need new nets, they leave bamboo frames in the jungle for the spiders to do their handiwork. It isn't long before the spiders have woven intricate webs onto the frames. These nets are waterproof and strong enough to be used for years.

FISH IN A BARREL: Jules Le Batteux of France had himself lowered into the water while inside a barrel that had a leather sleeve attached to it, allowing him to grab fish as they swam by.

TALL ORDER: Salmon fishermen on the Norwegian Sogne Fjord net their catch from balconies 70 feet above the water. When the net is full, the fishermen close it by yanking on a long line.

TROUT TRAP: This nine-and-half-inch brook trout (right), caught by Bobby Cunningham of Belfast, Maine, didn't actually break a record—it just got stuck in one.

CREEPY-CRAWLIES

HOMES EQUIPPED WITH AIR: Water spiders (above) stock their underwater nests with air by bringing it down in big bubbles from the surface.

EGGS-TREMELY SECURE: Malacosoma moths lay strings of eggs that they wind around the limbs of fruit trees. The eggs are glued so tightly that not even the heaviest storms can wash them away.

DO-IT-YOURSELF SURGERY: The Australian cockroach doesn't need wings because it lives underground, so when it reaches maturity, it bites off its own wings.

WALKING WOUNDED: The bronze locust can bleed at will, shedding big drops of blood whenever it's threatened.

ASBESTOS TOES: The fire beetle of Australia can walk through red-hot ashes.

CENSORSHIP: All the books on insects in the junior high school library in Moultrie, Georgia, were destroyed by termites.

HEAD CASE: The ostrich beetle stands on its head when threatened.

THE TERMINATOR: The Hercules beetle (below), which has a body the size of a fist, can grow up to eight inches long, including its horn. When males fight, they use their horn to pick up the enemy and fling him away.

6

Survivors

No one really knows what factors go into making a survivor. Is it toughness, optimism, or just plain luck? Here are some survival stories from the past and present files of Believe It or Not! After you've read them, perhaps you will be closer to finding an answer.

Believe It!

NATURAL DISASTERS

WHAT A BLAST: On August 27, 1883, the fiery volcanic explosion on Krakatoa, an island in Indonesia, was heard as far as 3,000 miles away. The first landing party to reach the ruined island found no survivors except for one red spider spinning its web.

FELL THROUGH THE CRACK: When an earthquake struck Alaska in 1964, Balas Ervin looked through a window to see the earth suddenly shoot upward 50 feet. A fissure had opened directly below the house, which plunged to the bottom of the crevasse. Luckily, Ervin escaped and even helped others to survive the most devastating American earthquake ever recorded.

GROUNDED: In 1953, several children were playing together when a tornado struck Worcester, Massachusetts. Caught in the vortex of the tornado, they were suddenly whisked into the air. It's a good thing their mothers were around to grab hold of them and drag them back to earth.

RECORD BREAKER: A tornado that struck Eldorado, Kansas, in 1958, sucked a woman through a window, swept her 60 feet through the air, and dropped her unharmed next to a broken record of "Stormy Weather." It then collapsed her house like a pack of cards.

FIRE AND BRIMSTONE: Mt. Pelee, on the island of Martinique in the French West Indies, erupted in 1902, killing 30,000 inhabitants of St. Pierre. One of the few survivors, Raoul Sarteret (below), a convicted murderer, saw the fiery eruption from his jail cell. He was eventually pardoned, and though he'd been burned and blinded by the volcanic gases, he went on to become a respected missionary.

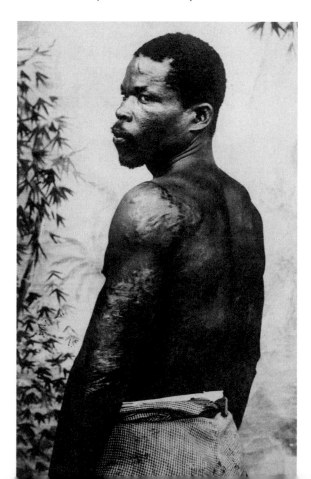

ROCK-A-BYE BABY: The flood that wiped out Johnstown, Pennsylvania, in 1889, killed thousands. But it spared one five-month-old infant who sailed all the way to Pittsburgh, 75 miles away, on the floorboards of a ruined house.

. . . ON THE TREETOP: After a tornado swept through Marshfield, Missouri, on April 18, 1880, a baby girl was found sleeping peacefully in the branches of a tall elm tree.

WAVE GOODBYE: In 1946, a Hawaiian family survived a tsunami—an enormous sea wave—that lifted their house off the foundation, swept it 200 feet, and deposited it in a cane field. All this, while their breakfast still simmered on the stove.

SLICE OF LIFE: In December of 1920, earthquakes caused massive landslides in China. In one valley, only three men survived when their entire farm split away from a cliff and floated intact down the valley on a river of watery clay.

FLOOD-GAIT: A flood overtook the streets of Edgemont, Ohio, in 1913. Flossie Lester, who was on foot, jumped aboard a horse-drawn carriage. When the turbulent waters caught up to the carriage and the horses broke harness, she swam after the horse and rode it to safety a mile and a half away.

LEAVE IT TO BEAVERS: In 1938, 60 beaver colonies in Stony Point, New York, fought back rampaging flood waters. The dams they built—many of which measured up to 600 feet long and 14 feet wide—were responsible for saving major highways, bridges, and hundreds of acres of valuable land.

SHIPWRECKED

ON THE BEAM: During a violent storm in the 19th century, Captain Benjamin Webster was swept overboard from the *Isaac Johnson* at the same time that a load of lumber on deck was cut loose. The captain landed on one of the beams. A moment later, a giant wave hurled that one board back onto the ship's deck with the captain astride it.

DEEPLY GRATEFUL: In 1939, Lieutenant Commander Francis Murphy spent 32 hours inside a United States submarine that sank in 243 feet of water in the Atlantic Ocean. He survived without injury.

CHARMED LIFE: Frank Tower swam away from three major shipwrecks: the *Titanic* in 1912, the *Empress of Ireland* in 1914, and the *Lusitania* (above) in 1915.

POD SQUAD: In 1991, a pod of dolphins protected a group of shipwrecked sailors from circling sharks off the coast of Florida.

REAL-LIFE JONAHS

ICE PACK: In 1969, nineteen sailors who survived when the U.S. *Polaris* was crushed by ice in the Arctic, were rescued in good health off the coast of Labrador, a peninsula in northern Canada. They had drifted 12,000 miles in over 196 days on an iceberg.

DEAD IN THE WATER: When the steamer *Mayflower* sank in Lake Kamaniskeg in Ontario, Canada, in 1912, there were just three survivors. They were saved by clinging to the coffin of a dead man.

DIDN'T MISS A BEAT: On September 8, 1860, 297 lives were lost when the *Lady Elgin* went down in Lake Michigan. But the *Lady Elgin*'s drummer boy, Charles Berung, saved himself by swimming to shore, using his drum as a life preserver.

THE RIGHT WAVELENGTH: In May of 1945, Lieutenant Commander Robert W. Goehring was swept off his ship by a mountainous wave during a storm. Just when he thought that all was lost, another giant wave tossed him back on board to safety.

LEFT A BAD TASTE: In 1771, the *Boston Post* reported that an American harpooner named Jenkins was swallowed by a sperm whale when it snapped his whale boat in two with one bite. Jenkins disappeared into the huge jaws but must have disagreed with the whale. It spat him out right away. Jenkins was not hurt.

WHALE OF A STORY: In 1891, James Bartley, a 35-year-old seaman on the British whaler *Star of the East*, was swallowed by a sperm whale. The whale was badly injured by harpoons and was found dead, floating on the surface, the next day. After hauling it aboard and slicing it open, the crew found Bartley, unconscious but still breathing, in the whale's stomach. He was delirious for days but recovered to describe his ordeal. Before passing out, he remembered seeing "a big ribbed canopy of light pink and white" above him, "a wall of soft flesh surrounding him and hemming him in," and then finding himself inside a water-filled sack among fish, some of which were still alive.

HEROES

HUMAN ANCHOR: On October 28, 1844, Mrs. Margaret Whyte of Aberdour, Scotland, was the only person onshore when the sailing ship *William Hope* was driven into the rocks by a raging storm. Whyte signaled the crew to throw her a line. But with no tree or post available, she tied the rope around her waist, dug her heels into the sand, and held the line taut against the pull of the tossing vessel while its entire crew of 12 came ashore one by one.

HANGIN' EIGHT: After a yacht capsized in rough waters off Newport Beach, California, in 1925, Hawaiian surfer Duke Kahanamoku, used his surfboard to single-handedly save the lives of eight passengers.

HUMAN BUS STOP: In December of 1996, bus driver Hamdija Osmana of Yugoslavia kept his bus from rolling over a cliff by jamming his legs under a wheel and stopping the vehicle. He saved 30 passengers.

HUMAN CORK: In January of 1870, Captain Thomas A. Scott brought his tug along-side a sinking ferryboat carrying hundreds of passengers in New York's North River. Using his own body, Captain Scott plugged a hole at the waterline of the listing boat. Scott's arm, which protruded through the hole, was severely lacerated by ice cakes, but all aboard the vessel were saved.

DID SWIMMINGLY: Nellie O'Donnell had never learned to swim. But in June of 1904, she saw an excursion boat, the *General Slocum*, sinking in New York's East River, with hundreds of women and children about to drown. With no thought for her own safety, she jumped into the water and saved ten lives before collapsing with exhaustion.

80

LEMONS TO LEMONADE

LUCKY STRIKE: In 1990, after becoming blind and deaf in a truck accident, Edwin Robinson of Falmouth, Maine, regained his sight and hearing when he was struck by lightning.

LUCKY BREAK: Opera star Etienne Laine got his training as a vegetable peddler in Paris, France, in the mid-1700s. One day, his voice came to the attention of the director of the Royal Academy of Music when his shouts of "Buy my asparagus" shattered a window in the director's office.

MUGGING FOR THE CAMERA: Movie actor Mel Gibson (right) won his leading role in the 1979 Australian film *Mad Max* because the director was searching for someone who looked weary, beaten, and scared. Gibson couldn't help but look the part, since he'd been mugged by three drunks the night before his screen test.

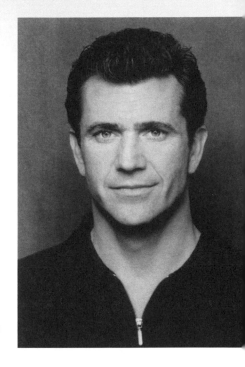

FEATHER-BRAINED CALL: John James Audubon (1785–1851), the noted bird illustrator, owed his success to his creditors. They took all his earthly possessions, but left his drawings, which they considered worthless. These drawings soon brought young Audubon fame and fortune.

HANDLE WITH CARE: Eighteen-month-old Renée Nivernas of Marseilles, France, was kidnapped from her home on August 4, 1908, and held for ransom aboard a yacht. A storm sank the ship and all eight kidnappers perished. But the little girl, sleeping in a makeshift cradle of packing cases, floated ashore at Cassis, France, unharmed.

TRAINS, PLANES, CARS, AND TRUCKS

DOUBLE-DECKER LANDING: In December of 1999, flight instructor Allen Van Gee was flying with student Barbara Yeninas in a Cessna 152 when a Piper Cadet airplane wedged itself on top of their plane. Van Gee successfully landed the two planes without causing any injuries.

ALL HUNG UP: In 1990, parachutist Michael Loeb got tangled during a jump and spent 20 minutes dangling 1,000 feet above the ground from a plane traveling 150 miles an hour.

IN A TAILSPIN: On a flight over Czechoslovakia in 1972, flight attendant Vesna Vulovic (below) was in the plane's tail when the plane exploded. She survived being thrown 33,000 feet to the ground.

TREE SERVICE: In 1997, Sergeant Cyril Jones, attempting to parachute into Sumatra, crashed into the forest and was suspended in the trees for 12 days. He survived by eating fruit brought to him by a monkey.

MILES TO GO . . . In 1969, Miles Lucas of New Jersey was thrown from his car after it crashed into the wall of a cemetery. Lucas walked away from the accident, but his car kept going. It didn't stop until it finally landed on a headstone. The name on the headstone was Miles Lucas—no relation.

NARROW ESCAPE: In 1993, all 163 passengers on an Air India flight that crashed and landed upside down (above) walked away from the wreckage before the plane burst into flames.

OFF THE BEATEN TRACK: In 1993, Nicole Bernier, age eight, of Willington, Connecticut, survived after a freight train passed over her body.

HAPPY LANDING: In 1972, U.S. skydiver Bob Hall jumped from a plane without a working parachute and fell 3,300 feet to the ground. He got up and walked away with only a broken nose.

TALL TAIL: Captain J.H. Hedley of Chicago, Illinois, fell out of a plane nearly three miles up in the air on January 6, 1918. Incredibly, just as the plane was making a steep vertical dive in line with his own fall, Hedley landed on the tail and made it to the ground, shaken but uninjured.

MAN AGAINST BEAST

WHAT A CROCK: In the late 1960s, when a crocodile clamped down on the leg of a citizen of Tamative, Madagascar, the man grabbed hold of the crocodile's leg and won his freedom and his life after an hour-long tug-of-war.

BOARD TO DEATH: In October of 1991, surfer John Ferreira of Stanford, California, survived a great white shark attack by jamming his surfboard into the shark's jaws and choking it to death.

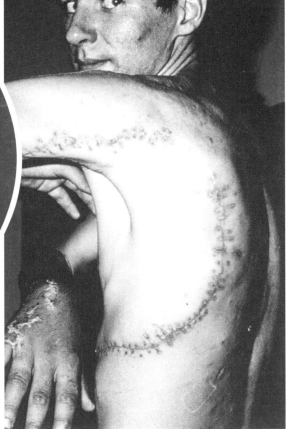

JAW BREAKER: In 1963 Rodney Fox (right) survived an attack by a 1,200 pound great white shark despite having sustained a wound that required 462 stitches.

THEY LIVED TO TELL THE TALE

NO YOLK! In 1947, two-year-old baby Zsuzsie of Yugoslavia fell from a third story window and landed in a basket of eggs carried by a passing peasant woman. The baby was unhurt—but the eggs got a little scrambled.

A LOT AT STAKE: In the mid-1990s, Neil Pearson slipped and fell, impaling himself on a metal pipe used as a stake to hold up plants. The stake went into his armpit, through his body, and out through his neck underneath his ear. X-rays revealed that the stake missed his veins and carotid artery, and every vital organ in its path. Doctors say that if this freak accident were a medical procedure, it would have been deemed too risky. All Pearson needed was five stitches to close up the wound. He was released from the hospital the same day.

HEADSTRONG: In 1930, Phineas P. Gage, of Cavendish, Vermont, survived an explosion that drove a 13-pound tamping iron through his brain. He lived for 12 years with a three and a half-inch hole in his skull.

WINDFALL: In March of 2000, Chris Grimes survived without serious injury after a freak gust of wind lifted him and the kite he was flying 24 feet into the air and carried him more than 600 feet before he landed on the other side of a river.

HUMAN HOCKEY PUCK: Hockey player Smoky Harris survived having his nose broken seven times, his jaw broken four times, his ribs broken 14 times, both knees broken, half a foot amputated, and 100 operations on his head.

BULLETPROOF MAN: On March 18, 1915, Wenseslao Moguel (right), of Mérida, Mexico, survived execution by a firing squad, even after the final bullet was fired at close range to ensure a quick death.

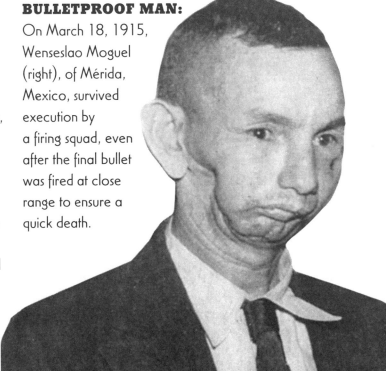

SURPRISE! Mrs. Margaret Erskine of Dryburgh, Scotland, was pronounced dead in 1574 and was buried in the family mausoleum. But that night, when the caretaker attempted to steal a ring from her finger, the dead woman sat up in her coffin and screamed. She recovered and lived for another 51 years.

HARD-KNOCK LIFE: At the age of 18, after traveling from Amsterdam to America in the 1600s, Penelope Van Princis was attacked by Native Americans. They killed her husband and left her for dead after fracturing her skull and shoving a spear through her body. She spent seven days in a hollow tree before being rescued, then went on to live for another 92 years. She was survived by 502 descendants when she finally died at the age of 110.

WRONG RECOVERY ROOM: In 1985, Eric Villet of Orléans, France, was officially declared dead after doctors failed to revive him with heart massage and oxygen. Incredibly, he started breathing three days later while lying in the morgue.

. . . HAD A GREAT FALL: In the spring of 1992, Garret Bartelt had gone to Valdez, Alaska, to compete in the World Extreme Skiing Championship. During the competition he took a tumble down the mountain's steepest slope. His fall was the longest in professional skiing history. Since extreme skiers wear no protective gear, the chances of Bartelt's escaping without serious injury were slim. But—Believe It or Not!—his injuries turned out to be minor, and two years later, he was back on the slopes, competing in another world championship.

DAREDEVIL DIVA: As one of the top powerboat racers in the world, Sarah Donohue's (right) combination of skill and looks made her a natural choice for a role in the James Bond movie, *The World Is Not Enough*. But her career almost came to an abrupt halt in September of 1999 after Donohue crashed while going over 100 miles an hour in a catamaran race. Her boating partner, Guiseppe Bevilaqua, escaped unharmed, but Donohue was knocked unconscious and trapped under the boat. After four minutes she was pulled from the wreckage and pronounced dead by the EMS. But Bevilaqua refused to give up and continued trying to revive her. His last-ditch effort paid off when Donohue began to cough up sea water. Miraculously, there was no brain damage, and after a difficult year of surgeries and physical therapy, Donohue's career is back on track.

THE HUMAN CANNONBALL: In 1782, an Indian holy man named Aruna, who angered the Sultan of Mysore, was twice stuffed into a cannon's barrel and fired into the air. He survived both times. The first time, he was blown 800 feet and landed on a soft canopy. The second, he fell without a scratch onto the thatched roof of a hut.

87

OVERCOMING ADVERSITY

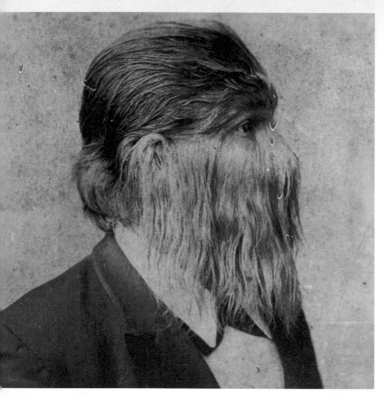

HAIRY PROBLEM: A condition called *hypertrichosis* causes uncontrolled hair growth. Also known as "werewolf syndrome," it is very rare. Jo Jo the Dog-Faced Boy (left), who suffered from the condition, was a popular Odditorium performer in the 1930s. Today brothers Larry and Danny Gomez, who live in a small village near Guadalajara, Mexico, also have hypertrichosis. Although they were teased unmercifully as children, they have found a way to capitalize on their condition. They call themselves the Wolf Brothers, and they are known all over the world for their skill as trapeze artists. Ironically, the knowledge gained by scientists who have studied them and 15 of their relatives who also have the disease, may lead to a cure for baldness.

BLIND SPOT: Ken Moss was blinded in an accident while working as a traffic cop in Scarborough, England. But far from letting his handicap get him down, Moss decided to fulfill his dream of becoming a race-car driver. At first, his son took him out on private roads. Then former race-car driver Tony Pond took over and gave Moss 600 hours of professional training. A car was custom-designed for him, equipped with its own navigational system, special gear shift, and a computer that could be attached to a high-tech helmet to help him steer. On the day of his first race, Moss reached a speed of 131 miles per hour, making him the world's first blind race-car driver.

HALF WOMAN, HALF SUPER-WOMAN: Rose Siggins gets around on a skateboard, propelling herself at breakneck speed with her arms. Born without legs, pelvis, or spine below her rib cage, this engaging woman does not dwell on what she's missing. She chooses instead to focus on what she has— a lot by anyone's standards. Siggins, who is an auto mechanic, met her husband at the automotive parts store where he works. Besides fixing cars, she swims, does housework, and takes care of the baby she gave birth to at great risk to herself. Siggins is living proof that a positive attitude contributes more to a successful life than any other gifts we are born with.

REAL-LIFE TARZAN: At just two years old, John Ssebunya of Uganda got so upset when his mother was murdered, he ran off into the forest that surrounded his small village. No one knew if he was dead or alive. Years of bloody civil war in the area meant that a missing person was hardly a rare occurrence. But John was alive and living with a family of monkeys that taught him to survive on fruits, nuts, and berries.

Four years later, Millie Sseba was gathering firewood when she saw the youngster in a tree. She got aid from other villagers who helped pull the frightened six-year-old to the ground. They took him to an orphanage where for the first time, John was exposed to life's modern conveniences. That first night, his new brothers and sisters prepared a bed for him, but he was found the next morning cowering in a corner. It didn't take long, however, for this bright little boy to learn to read and write and make lots of new friends.

Today, John plays soccer and sings with a children's choir that takes him all around the world. But he has not forgotten his old friends, the monkeys, with whom he still shares an unspoken language. To this day, monkeys that run from other people feel perfectly at ease in John's presence.

BLIND LEADING THE BLIND: Dan Kish (above) is blind. But that doesn't keep him from doing anything he wants. Fiercely independent by nature, Kish does not like to rely on others to help him find his way around. That's why he became interested in sonar, also known as echolocation.

Sonar is the method that bats, dolphins, and other animals with poor vision use to navigate their surroundings. Kish saw no reason why human beings couldn't use sonar to find their way around as well. So he developed a human version of echolocation that involves making a clicking noise with his tongue. He listens carefully as the sound bounces off surrounding objects and returns back to him as an echo. Then Kish interprets the sounds to figure out the size, shape, and distance of everything in his immediate environment. He uses echolocation to do his errands, and even to ride his dirtbike.

Kish has found this method so helpful to him in his daily life that he now teaches other blind people to use it. After only a few hours of instruction, his students can navigate quite easily. One of his students was able to accurately and precisely identify everything in an environment he had never been to before.

7
Home, Hearth & Peculiar Places

The place Robert Ripley called home was a 29-room mansion on BION (an acronym for Believe It or Not!), his very own island near Mamaroneck, New York. Ripley's love of architecture was reflected in his travels. If there was an unusual building to see, he would go out of his way to find it.

Believe It!

HOME SWEET HOME

SMARTEST: A computerized house at Ahwatukee, Arizona, can turn on its own lights, talk to it owners, and help prepare a grocery list.

MOST ECONOMICAL: A home built beneath an abandoned opal mine in Australia provides more than shelter. Every now and then, the owners dig gems from its walls for a little financial help.

MOST SPITEFUL: A home at Lexington Avenue and 82nd Street in New York City was four stories tall and only five feet wide at each end. It was built by Joseph Richardson for the sole purpose of blocking his next-door neighbor's view.

CROOKEDEST: Herman de Waal's home in Utrecht, Holland, has no straight walls.

MOST WELCOMING: Once a private home in Stirlingshire, England, this house (above) is shaped like a pineapple, the symbol for hospitality. Now the Pineapple House is rented out for the holidays by a British building preservation charity known as the Landmark Trust.

MOST EXTRAVAGANT: A pyramid-shaped structure owned by a Waukegan, Illinois, developer, is one-ninth the scale of Egypt's Great Pyramid. The home is covered with 24-karat gold plate and decorated in an Egyptian theme.

FLATTEST: An architectural phenomenon in Alexandria, Egypt, is a three-room house that was once attached to a wall.

TRICKIEST: In the Bayswater section of London, England, 23 Leinster Gardens appears to be a handsome four-story apartment building. It is actually a facade painted on a cement wall to conceal the entrance to a subway tunnel.

MOST BREAKABLE: A home (below) built on Prince Edward Island in Canada by Eduoard Arsenault was constructed entirely from glass bottles.

SHADIEST: The home of Alfred Rexrothin of Lohr, Germany, was built around a 241-foot-high fir tree that extends through its roof.

DAMPEST: Baldassare Forestiere once worked as a sandhog, helping to build New York City's subways. When he moved to Fresno, California, he used a pick and shovel to dig himself a 35-room home, with a mile of connecting tunnels. It took him 37 years to complete his home.

MOST INTERNATIONAL: A house near Sweetgrass, Montana, has its bedroom in the United States and its kitchen in Canada.

MOST DURABLE: Justo Rosito of Alcolea del Pinar, Spain, spent 22 years carving his seven-room house (below) out of solid rock. He included built-in benches, shelves, and even a fireplace. The Spanish government was so impressed with his effort that they gave him the five acres surrounding the home free of charge.

MOST COLORFUL: One side of this apartment house (above) owned by Mark Van Noppen and Tyler Roberts in Providence, Rhode Island, was given an elaborate color-by-number look that included crayon scrawls and three 17-foot crayons.

STOP, THIEF! The two lower floors of a three-story house on Herkimer Street in Albany, New York, were stolen.

MOST SOLE-FULL: A house in Kamala Nehru Park in Mumbai, India, is shaped like a giant shoe.

TASTIEST: A gingerbread house built in the Cleveland, Ohio, convention center was 19 feet high, had three rooms, a fireplace, a chimney, and 7,000 gingerbread bricks. Building it required 2,200 pounds of flour, 2,700 pounds of powdered sugar, 3,000 egg whites, and 1,965 pounds of other ingredients.

MOST PORTABLE: Houses used by people of northern Nigeria are merely large mats sewn together in the shape of a hut, which can be shifted easily from place to place.

DID YOU KNOW . . .

. . . that the first apartment house (above) was built by Rutherford Stuyvesant in New York City on 18th street? It cost $100,000 and a lot of teasing. It was nicknamed "Stuyvesant's Folly" because it was felt no one would be willing to share a home with strangers.

. . . that John Howard Payne, author of "Home, Sweet Home," never had a home? He wandered the globe all his life, finally dying penniless in Tunisia.

. . . that nails were so prized in Colonial America that old houses were burned down to recover them?

. . . that Gracie Mansion in New York City—once used as a storage facility, a public restroom, and an ice cream stand—is now the only official mayor's residence in the United States?

COME ON INN

FOR THE BIRDS: The Bostonian Hotel in Boston, Massachusetts, once reserved a $250 room for the exclusive use of a mother sparrow that laid four eggs on the room's balcony (above).

COLD COMFORT: The Ice Hotel (below), 400 miles north of Stockholm, is the most popular and well-known resort in Sweden. It is made entirely of ice. Every year it takes 20 sculptors 23 days to complete the hotel, which includes a theater and a chapel where many couples have taken their vows. There are 37 master suites, each designed by a different artist, and special thrones carved for the king and queen of Sweden who vacation there every year. The temperature inside is a downright toasty 5°F compared to the outside, which is 50°F below zero. The only part of the hotel that is wired for electricity is the bar, because beverages must be refrigerated to keep them from freezing. The hotel is booked solid from October to May. After May, it just melts away, leaving a huge puddle, the only evidence it ever existed.

IT TOOK A VILLAGE: The entire Balkan fishing village of St. Stephen (above), in Montenegro, was converted into a resort hotel. The old homes of peasants became luxury suites.

DOG-GONE EXCLUSIVE: The White Topps Hotel in Bournemouth, England, only accepts guests who are accompanied by dogs.

TAKE THE ELEVATOR: The Hotel du Lac, in Tunis, Tunisia, is shaped like an upside down staircase.

TOP OF THE LINE: Treetops, a resort in Kenya, Africa, was built atop a group of chestnut trees so that guests would have spectacular views of the wildlife.

FOUR-BIDDEN: Hotels in China rarely have a fourth floor because the character for the number four is the same as the character for death.

DEEP SLEEP: Jules' Undersea Lodge (below) is a hotel built below the ocean's surface off Florida's Key Largo. Guests can view marine life and scuba divers while they relax in bed.

ASTONISHING STRUCTURES

STRAW PALACE: The Alfalfa Palace in Fallon, Nevada, built in 1915 to house the agricultural exhibit at the state fair, was constructed entirely from 54 tons of hay.

STAIRWAY TO HEAVEN: The Miraculous Staircase, so named because it was built without supports of any kind, can be found in Santa Fe, New Mexico.

EXTRA FIRM: Stone beds carved in the solid cliffs of the Sahara Desert make cool resting places for travelers who would otherwise have to spend the night on the hot desert sand.

DON'T GET LOST: The Skydome Stadium (above) in Toronto, Canada, is big enough to hold over 1,200 elephants or eight Boeing 747 airplanes.

CANINE CASTLE: A 70-foot-high tower in the Castle of Chinon, France, was especially built by King Philip II for his dogs.

HEAD-QUARTERS: The Armour-Stiner house (left) in Irvington-on-Hudson, represents a human brain. Its rooms were laid out according to the principles of phrenology, the pseudoscience that maintains that bumps on the head have an effect on personality.

IT'S MELTING! A building in Odeillo, France, designed to tap solar energy for heat and light, looks as if it's actually dissolving.

FISH OUT OF WATER: Built in the shape of a fish, the National Freshwater Fishing Hall of Fame (above), in Hayward, Wisconsin, is half a city block long and four-and-a-half stories high.

PERFECT PITCH: Designed 2,000 years ago by Greek architects, a theatre in Aspendos, Turkey, is so acoustically perfect that every word spoken on its stage can be heard with clarity in any of its 13,000 seats.

SHELL SHOCK-PROOF: The Castillo de San Marco in St. Augustine, Florida, a star-shaped fort, is constructed partially of sea shells. Despite numerous attacks on it, it has never been taken.

LAUGHING WALLS: Within the Whispering Gallery in the dome of Gol-Gumaz in Bijapur, India, the sound of laughter echoes 20 times while all other sounds echo no more than ten.

GIFT FROM THE SEA: This tiny chapel on the Isle of Guernsey in Great Britain (below) is made entirely of sea shells.

DID YOU KNOW . . .

. . . that Reykjavik, Iceland (above), has no problem with air pollution because its buildings are heated by hot springs?

. . . that Hollywood, California's film capital, was named after an English racehorse?

. . . that the Oklahoma gold rush created two cities, each with a population of 10,000, in a single day? Their names are Guthrie and Oklahoma City.

. . . that the first city to be lit entirely by electricity was Aurora, Illinois?

. . . that Oraibi, built in Arizona by the Hopi Indians in the 1100s, is the oldest continuously inhabited settlement in the United States?

. . . that Canada's coastline equals a distance of more than twice the circumference of Earth?

FAIR-WEATHER CHURCH: The Madonna Chapel of Bayou Goula, Louisiana, is just large enough to accommodate the priest during mass. The worshippers must remain outside.

CARVED IN STONE: The largest Buddha in the world (below) stands at the top of a mountain in China. The Giant Buddha of Leshan is 230 feet tall. It was carved out of the cliff side on the Lingyun mountain during the eighth century. It is so staggeringly large that more than 100 people can sit between its enormous feet. As a local saying goes, "The mountain is a Buddha, the Buddha is a mountain."

FINE DINING

BARK AVENUE: A restaurant in Nice, France, serves gourmet dinners—including appetizer, main course, and dessert—to dogs.

FROG LEGS, ANYONE? Something you might expect to be served at a place like Toed Inn—a restaurant in Los Angeles, California, that was shaped like a huge toad.

ON A ROLL: The largest restaurant in the world, the Royal Dragon, in Bangkok, Thailand, can seat 5,000 people at one time. To speed up the service, guests are served by 1,200 waiters on roller skates.

WORM YOUR WAY IN: The Insect Club in Washington, D.C., serves cricket meatloaf and mealworm wontons.

SNAKEBITES: In restaurants in China, live reptiles are frequently brought to the tables of diners so they can choose their own snakes to have for dinner (above).

DINING FOR PEARLS: When dining out with their parents, little Timothy and Samantha Aurelia, of Glens Falls, New York, found ten pearls in the marinated mussels they ordered for dinner.

OFF THE BEATEN TRACK

DON'T FORGET YOUR BOOTS: Dede, a village in the bed of the Yangtze River in China, is habitable only three months of the year because it is under water during the other nine.

INTOXICATING AMBIENCE: In the market place of Kitzingen, Germany, houses are built out of mortar mixed with wine.

CONE HOMES: A community (below) in Cappadocia, Turkey, consists of homes created by the lava flow of a now-extinct volcano. The cone-shaped rock formations were hollowed out to be used as homes and chapels by early Christians. Now inhabited by Turkish farmers, many of the homes have as many as ten floors.

SOFT ROCK: The 30,000 homes in the borough of Santiago (above), in Guadix, Spain, are all caves carved into rock that is so soft it can be cut like cheese. Each home is equipped with electric lights and tiled floors. Their main advantage is that they seem to have a natural climate-control that keeps residents warm in winter and cool in summer.

A TOWN ON THE GO: A community in western Australia, in the heart of the lumber and gold-mining areas, has its homes, shops, post office, and police station mounted on railroad cars.

KEEPING AFLOAT: In Aquapolis, a community off Okinawa, Japan, the residents live on a floating structure that looks very much like an oil rig when seen from the shore.

TIGHT SQUEEZE: Kitty Witches Row in Yarmouth, England, is so narrow that at one point it is only 1 foot 11.5 inches wide.

SOCIAL CLIMBERS: Sewell, a town on the mountain of El Teniente in Chile, has a population of 6,000 but no streets or vehicles. Since its sidewalks consist entirely of stairways, people must climb up or down to visit their neighbors.

BARE BONES: Mezhirich, a town in the Ukraine, was built 15,000 years ago. Its houses are made entirely out of the bones of mammoths.

PEAK EXPERIENCE: In 1435, a community of 29 houses in the French Alps was shifted from one mountain peak to another at the request and expense of Henri Lacaris, so that the woman he loved would live nearer to him.

BELIEVE IT OR NOT!

Norwegian viking Floke Velgedarsson discovered Iceland in 865 using three ravens as his only navigational guide. He had noticed that ravens always came to Norway from the north, so he released one bird each time he needed to check his position.

So many people live in China that it takes six million census takers ten days to count them all.

All 42 residents of Sentinel Butte, North Dakota, have keys to Albert Oldon's gas pump so they can pump their own gas when he's not working.

A sign in Markle, Indiana, states: Welcome to Markle—Home of 902 Happy People and 4 Grouches.

A statue, erected in Givayaquil, Ecuador, to honor poet José Joaquín Olmedo, is actually a statue of English poet Lord Byron, bought second-hand.

NAME-DROPPING

SIGN LANGUAGE: Ripley poses in a Welsh town with the second longest name in the world (above). The longest name belongs to a town in New Zealand.

TWO EGG, a town in Florida, was named for a system of barter used in the area after the Civil War, when two eggs were regularly traded for a bag of tobacco or sugar.

ED AND UZ are the shortest place names in the United States. Both towns are in Kentucky.

SLOVENSKANARODNAPODPORNAJE-DNOTA is a town in Pennsylvania. It has one of the longest names in the United States, but it covers only 500 acres and has only 11 residents, one mailbox, and one pay phone.

ONOVILLE, NEW YORK, was given this name because each time someone suggested a name at a town council meeting, the person was greeted by a chorus of "Oh, no!"

SHOW LOW is the name of a town in Arizona that was won in a game of chance. Two frontiersmen, dissolving a partnership, agreed the town site would go to the one who drew the low card.

PIG'S EYE was the former name of St. Paul, the capital of Minnesota.

SNOWFLAKE, a town in Arizona, was named after Erastus Snow and William Flake.

AND DON'T FORGET TO VISIT . . .
- Odd, West Virginia.
- Peculiar, Missouri.
- Ding Dong, Texas.

AND LAST, BUT NOT LEAST
- No Place, England.

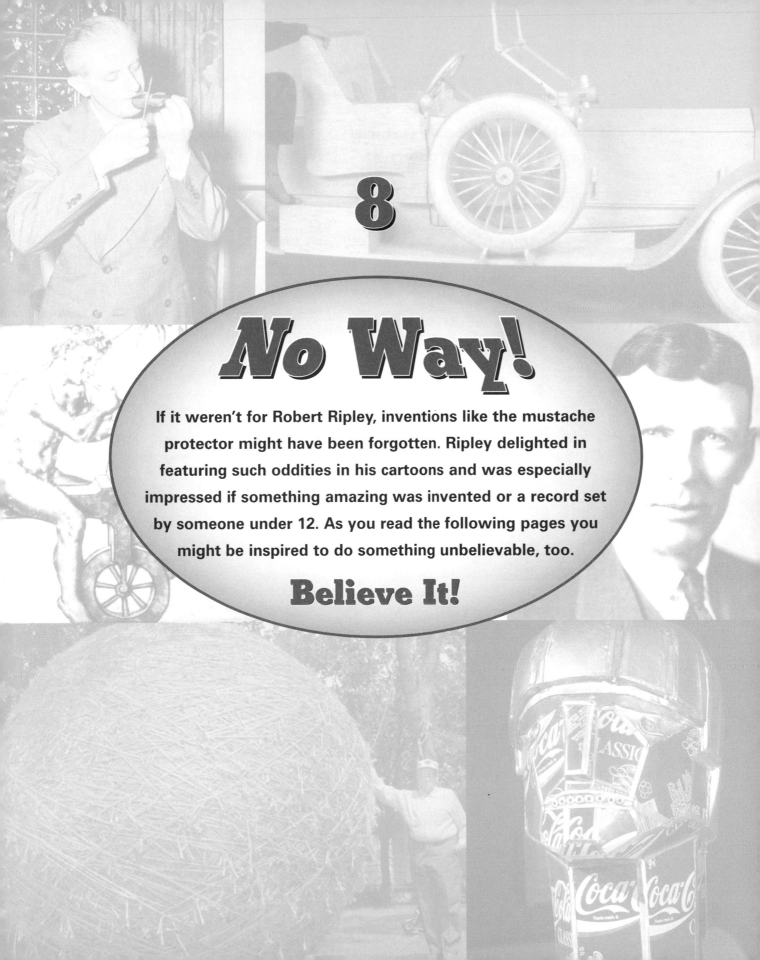

8

No Way!

If it weren't for Robert Ripley, inventions like the mustache protector might have been forgotten. Ripley delighted in featuring such oddities in his cartoons and was especially impressed if something amazing was invented or a record set by someone under 12. As you read the following pages you might be inspired to do something unbelievable, too.

Believe It!

FLIGHTS OF FANCY

Some of Ripley's favorite oddities were made by people who went to great lengths to fashion extraordinary works from ordinary objects.

WOOD YOU BELIEVE?
How did Joseph Shagena of Sebring, Florida, pierce a bottle with a wooden arrow (right) without shattering the glass? He donated this and other creative wonders to Ripley's, provided that the secret to their creation was sealed inside a vault. The secret remains locked away to this day.

CHAIN REACTION: Robert Ripley was so impressed with the continuous chain whittled by H.T. Stewart from a single 20- by 1-foot plank that he used himself to display it (above).

EYE STRAIN: That's what Harold Blahnik of Kewanee, Wisconsin, must have had after threading an ordinary sewing needle with 93 strands of thread (right).

MATCH SCHTICK: In 1983, Reg Pollard built a replica of a 1907 Rolls Royce Silver Ghost (above) out of more than one million matchsticks.

MATCHLESS: After Fritz Meng, of Bad Homburg, Germany, built a violin (above) out of 8,000 matchsticks, he claimed that its tone was beyond compare.

TOAST OF THE TOWN: Tadhiko Okawa used burnt toast to re-create Leonardo da Vinci's Mona Lisa (above) and other works of art.

CAN YOU BELIEVE IT? Created by Theresa Tozer in 1982, this huge metal sculpture (right) was made out of flattened soda cans.

TINY TREASURES

COIN OF A KIND: No one would ever guess that this ordinary-looking penny (right) has a slide-out drawer with a photograph of the famous collector of miniatures, Jules Charbneau, inside.

MINI MASTERPIECE: This miniature replica of the Crucifixion of Christ (below) was painted by Argentinian Manuel Andrada on the surface of a dime.

LITTLE SHOTS: The world's smallest cameras (above) are built by master miniaturist Harvey Libowitz of Brooklyn, New York. They stand 5.75 inches high on a collapsible tripod, and can actually take pictures.

WASTE NOT, WANT NOT: Fashioned out of laundry lint by Slater Barron in the 1980s, these sushi offerings (below) do not need to be refrigerated.

WRITER'S CRAMP: Convicted forger A. Schiller engraved a gold pin (above) with all 65 words and 254 letters of the Lord's Prayer. The head of the pin measured 47/1000ths of an inch. Under magnification, it can be seen that every word and line is perfectly spaced and every letter is completely legible.

MINIATURE MARVELS: Willard Wigan's sculptures are invisible to the naked eye. You need a very good microscope to see his Snow White and the Seven Dwarfs perched in the eye of a sewing needle (below), his copy of Mt. Rushmore on the sharp tip of a pencil, and his polar bear sitting on a single granule of sugar. Microsurgeons come from far and wide to observe Willard in his studio, hoping to learn the secret of his super-steady hands. These microsculptures may be seen by visiting The Impossible MicroWorld Museum in Bath, England, or by visiting the museum's website at www.theimpossiblemicroworld.com.

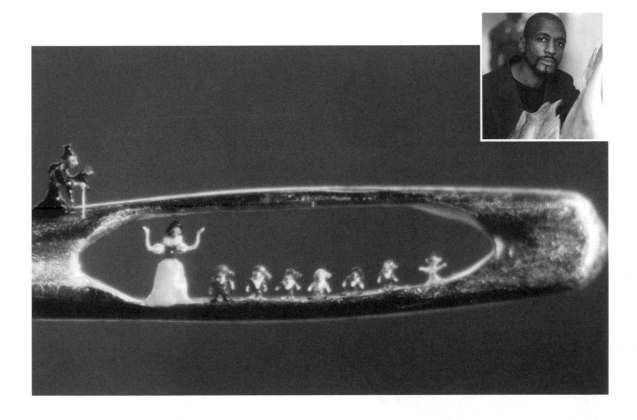

BABY BILLIARD TABLE: In addition to mini cameras, Harvey Libowitz built a fully functional miniature pool table (below). But it works better if you're an elf.

ITSY BITSY TEA SET: This gold tea set, which fits inside a gold locket (below), is a miniature marvel from the Jules Charbneau collection. Inside the locket's lid is Charbneau's miniature business card.

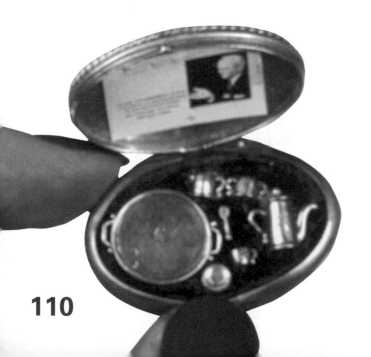

TINY TUNES: In the 1930s, Robert L. Ratte gave a live concert on his 5.5 inch mini-violin (above) on Ripley's radio show.

SO BIG!

COLOSSAL COLLAGE: Standing 25 feet tall and 20 feet wide, this reproduction of Vincent van Gogh's famous self-portrait (left) was created by Dutch artist Cornel Bierens from 3,000 postcards, each featuring a painting by Van Gogh.

GIANT DOLL HOUSE: A model of Sleeping Beauty's castle was built by Michael S. Di Persio of Bradley Beach, New Jersey. It stood eight feet tall and had 33 floors, 1,637 windows, 184 doors, and 752 steps.

MEGA PRINTER: Manufactured in Japan, the world's biggest computer printer weighs 14 tons, and is nearly 70 feet long and nine feet high. It can print an entire four-color, 50-foot-wide billboard in one motion.

HAD A BALL: It must have taken Francis Johnson of Darwin, Minnesota, quite a while to collect all the string to make this enormous ball of twine (right). It took nothing less than a railroad jack to move it from his yard to its current location, across the street from the Stringball Café.

WHAT ELSE COULD THEY DO?

What's in a name? A lot apparently. The names and the lives led by the following people bear an uncanny relationship.

H.M. Balmer (above) was a funeral director in Fort Collins, Colorado.

Iccolo Miccolo played the piccolo for the Los Angeles Philharmonic Orchestra.

Miss Birdie Snyder married C. Canary and became **Birdie Canary**.

Perhaps it was best to ignore the orders of **Dr. Besick**, a doctor in Chicago, Illinois.

The **Clipper** brothers worked as barbers in Bakersfield, California.

Mr. Thrift of Keepit, Australia, won the $30,000 first prize in a lottery.

Signature (right) of **D. Sharp**, radio tenor.

Dr. H.A. Toothacre worked as a dentist for the Burlington, Iowa, Independent School District.

B.F. Parsons was a parson who lived in the parsonage on Parson Street in Sarna, Michigan.

A.C. Current was an electrical contractor in Tontogany, Ohio. His son's name? **D.C. Current**.

Greg Lawless (right) was a police officer.

DID YOU KNOW. . .

. . . that many people believe that Mother Goose was a real person, not an imaginary character? Her maiden name was Elizabeth Foster. She married Isaac Goose in 1693, and later wrote her famous rhymes for her grandchildren.

TALENT TO SPARE

SKETCHY ART: By manipulating his Etch A Sketch so that he could form curved lines instead of just straight ones, George Vlosich (left) created a perfect replica of the Capitol Building in Washington, D.C., when he was just a little boy. Years later, his skill began to pay off. After the magnetic chips in the back of the toy are removed, his Etch A Sketch art fetches up to $3,000 apiece. Best of all, Vlosich has met some of his favorite celebrities by creating portraits like the one shown below. So far, he has met Michael Jordan, Sandy and Roberto Alomar, Cal Ripken Jr., David Robinson, and President Clinton, to name just a few.

PEE WEE PICASSO: Georgie Pocheptsov (left) started drawing when he was just a baby. At seven, he was selling paintings like the one above for $11,000—and there is a 20-month waiting list to buy them.

WAY TO GO

STRONG SUIT: Nature photographer Tony Hurtubise wanted to observe grizzly bears without putting himself in danger, so he invented a suit that is 50 times stronger and 85 percent lighter than steel. To test it out, he stood in front of a brick wall while a car suspended on wires was swung into his chest like a pendulum. The 35,000-pound impact decimated the brick wall, yet left Tony unharmed (above).

SEW CLEVER: Scientists in Great Britain have developed a tiny sewing machine that can be swallowed by a patient and then manipulated from outside the body to stitch damaged tissue.

SPOTTING SPOT: A battery-powered dog collar that glows in the dark was invented in 1989 by six-year-old Collin Hazen of Fargo, North Dakota.

COOL IDEA: In 1863, Chester Greenwood invented earmuffs when he was just 15.

NOISE FLASH: In 1989, when he was eight years old, Brian Berlinski of Clifton, New Jersey, invented a silent car horn for the hearing impaired—a light on the dashboard flashes at the sound of a honking horn.

THE REAL REAL McCOY: The son of slaves, Elijah McCoy was an inventor who lived in the1800s. His inventions worked so well that his name inspired a new phrase. To this day when nothing else will do, people still insist on having "the real McCoy."

FASTEN-ATING IDEA: Velcro was invented in 1940 by Swiss scientist George de Maestral after studying burrs he found clinging to his clothing.

INTO THE DUSTBIN

FOLLOWING SUITS: Invented by Mark Woehrer of Nebraska, Tag-a-long, the robotic suitcase carrier that follows its owner wherever he or she goes, has yet to catch on.

STIFF UPPER LIP: In 1872, Eli J.F. Randolph of New York patented the mustache protector. Meant to keep the mustache neat and tidy while eating and drinking, it was a hard rubber device with prongs that fit into the nostrils. To date, it has not yet found its market.

EDISON'S FOLLIES: Thomas A. Edison (below) was granted 1,093 United States patents. However, not all were winners, for instance, his perpetual cigar and his cement furniture.

WAIL OF A DUD: Patented in 1971, an electrical device designed to put a baby to sleep with a series of regular pats on the bottom seemed to make the baby cry harder.

DULL IDEA: Jack Broughton, the inventor of boxing gloves, also invented the pea knife to prevent peas from rolling off the knife while eating.

WHEELS, WINGS, AND WHIMSICAL THINGS . . .

DETAILS, DETAILS: A flying automobile was flown successfully in the United States in 1947, but crashed because the pilot had forgotten to fill the gas tank.

SUB CYCLE: In 1896, Alvary Templo built an underwater bicycle. Air carried in a submarine and piped to Templo's helmet enabled him to stay underwater up to six hours.

KITE OVER MIGHT: In 1826, a light carriage pulled by kites won a race against the Duke of Gloucester, who drove an ordinary carriage pulled by four horses.

BALLOONATIC: In 1982, Larry Walters rose three miles in a lawn chair held up by 24 helium balloons.

HOLY SPOKES: In the 1600s, a bicycle was featured in a stained-glass window (below) in Stoke Poges, England—nearly 200 years before it was invented.

PLAY WITH YOUR FOOD: The sandwich was named after the Earl of Sandwich, who invented it so he could eat a meal without interrupting his card game.

FRONT-WHEEL DRIVE: A dogmobile, patented in the United States in 1870, was propelled by two dogs running inside a cage inside the front wheels.

ROLL-PLAYING: In 1760, Joseph Merlin, a Belgian musician, invented roller skates. He demonstrated them by skating across a ballroom while playing the violin.

KIDS ON TRACK: A children's railway in Harbin, Manchuria, has an engine and four coaches. It runs on seven miles of track through a public park and is operated entirely by children under the age of 14.

SLOW AND STEADY: Used by General George Washington in the Revolutionary War, the first American submarine was called the Turtle.

WHAT TOOK SO LONG? A California mechanic built an eight-foot-high metal unicycle from a design drawn 500 years ago by Leonardo da Vinci.

LAND SAILING: In China, heavy wheelbarrows are equipped with sails to make them easier to push.

BELIEVE IT OR NOT!

Austrian botanist Gregor Johann Mendel, who discovered the laws of heredity, couldn't pass the exam to become a science teacher.

An empty Boeing 747 jumbo jet weighs as much as 67 elephants.

The French TGV regularly reaches its top speed of 320 miles per hour, making it the fastest passenger train in the world.

The East Japan Railway is used by over 16 million people each day, making it the busiest railway in the world.

An advertisement for bicycles in the late 1800s described them as "an ever saddled horse which eats nothing."

Before the invention of the microchip, computers were so big they had to be kept in special rooms.

George Washington Carver, inventor of more than 300 uses for peanuts, sweet potatoes, and soybeans, was kidnapped as a baby and ransomed for a horse.

According to a decision of the United States Court of Customs and Patent Appeals, an invention is "sometimes . . . simply the product of sheer stupidity."

RECORD BREAKERS

FLYING HIGH: Sixteen-year-old Katrina Mumaw (left) is still too young to fly alone. At age five, she started flying in a 1929 open cockpit plane at a local airshow. Since then she has flown just about every type of aircraft, from a Goodyear blimp to a Russian Mig. She made history at age 11 when she flew a Mig jet in Russia past Mach 1.3—an incredible 940 miles per hour—and became the youngest person ever to break the sound barrier. Mumaw hopes to become a fighter pilot and ultimately be on the first manned mission to Mars.

REINVENTING THE WHEEL: Canadian unicyclist Kris Holm (right) thinks nothing of riding along a felled 20-foot tree or circling the rim of a 200-foot cliff. That's small stuff. Another record-breaking stunt included riding within four inches of a 2,000-foot cliff and leaping six feet across a crevasse thousands of feet deep—all without brakes and with nothing to hold on to. Though what Holm does is strictly for extreme athletes only, unicycling is fantastic fun at a much safer level, too, and he would love to see the sport catch on with young people.

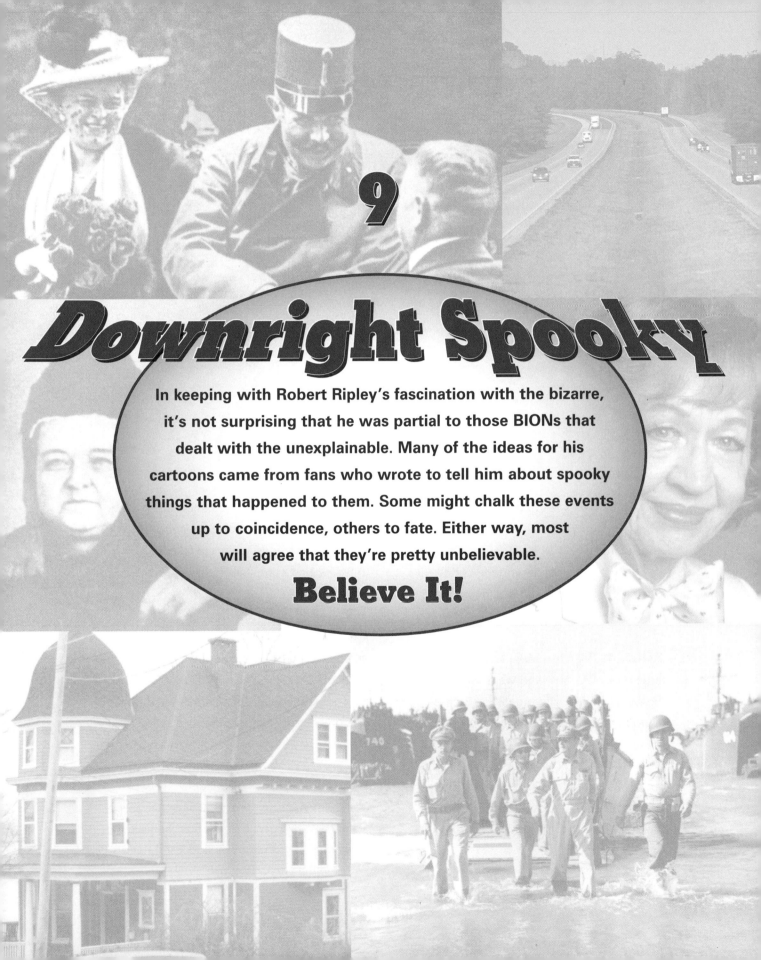

9

Downright Spooky

In keeping with Robert Ripley's fascination with the bizarre, it's not surprising that he was partial to those BIONs that dealt with the unexplainable. Many of the ideas for his cartoons came from fans who wrote to tell him about spooky things that happened to them. Some might chalk these events up to coincidence, others to fate. Either way, most will agree that they're pretty unbelievable.

Believe It!

COINCIDENCE?

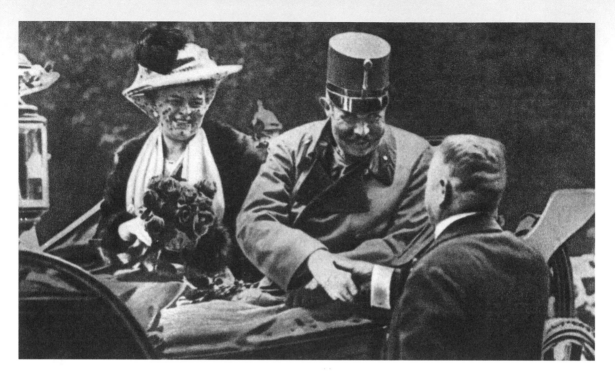

POSSESSED! The car in which Archduke Franz Ferdinand (above) of Austria was assassinated is now in a Vienna museum. The archduke's assassination started World War I. Since then, the same car was in nine accidents before it was taken off the road.

HUGH WHO? In 1664, 1785, and 1820, three unrelated men who were the sole survivors of three different disasters at sea were all named Hugh Williams.

SHARED FATE: Brothers Erskine L. Ebbin and Neville Ebbin of Bermuda died one year apart after being struck by the same taxi, driven by the same driver, and carrying the same passenger.

CHECKMATE: A bank customer who tried to cash a check in Monroe Township, New Jersey, was arrested when the teller turned out to be the Linda Brandimato to whom the check was made out.

CREDIT DENIED: A customer presented a stolen credit card to cashier Diane Klos in an Irvington, New Jersey, store. Klos recognized the card immediately since it belonged to her. Klos and her boss chased the thief to the street, where she was apprehended by two policemen.

RINGMASTER: While Stephen Law of Markham, Ontario, was hunting in five feet of water for a ring lost by his father, he found a topaz ring his grandmother had lost 41 years earlier in the very same lake.

ATE HIS FISH AND HIS WORDS: Moses Carlton, a wealthy ship magnate of Wiscasset, Maine, threw his gold ring into the Sheepscot River and boasted, "There is as much chance of my dying a poor man as there is of ever finding that ring again." A few days later, he found the ring in a fish served to him in a restaurant. Carlton's fortunes changed almost immediately. President Madison placed an embargo on American ships, Carlton went bankrupt, and, sure enough, he died a poor man.

TRUNK-ATED ENGAGEMENT: The schooner *Susan and Eliza* was wrecked in a storm off Cape Ann, Massachusetts. Aboard was one of the ship owner's daughters, Susan Hichborn, on her way to her wedding in Boston. All 33 passengers perished, and no trace of the ship was ever found, except for a trunk bearing Susan's initials and containing her possessions. The trunk washed ashore at the feet of her waiting fiancé.

PLAYING FAVORITES: In 1938, a hurricane damaged or destroyed 6,923 churches along the East Coast of the United States, but spared all the synagogues and Episcopal churches.

REKINDLED KIN: Identical twins Mark Newman and Jerry Levey, adopted by different families five years after they were born in 1954, did not meet again until 1986. Both grew up to be volunteer firefighters and found each other entirely by chance while attending a firefighters' convention.

FLAKY SUMMER: Snow fell three times in New England in July 1816, fulfilling a prediction made in that year's edition of *The Old Farmer's Almanac* that had been inserted as a prank.

SPIRITS, PROPHECIES, AND DREAMS

CAT-ASTROPHE: At five o'clock on the morning of November 2, 1951, a woman named Nova Churchill woke up crying, "I dreamed a black panther jumped on my mother and killed her." A phone call received later that day confirmed Nova's dream. Her mother had had a heart attack while dusting a ceramic panther—at the exact moment Nova awoke from her dream.

ARRESTING VISIONS: Chris Robinson (right) has been called "a force to be reckoned with" by Scotland Yard. He is a janitor in Bedforshire, England, by day and a psychic at night. He had a dream about a hotel where five terrorists were planning atrocities that resulted in their arrest at that very hotel. Another dream foreshadowed an explosion at Bournemouth Pier. Once alerted, the police were able to locate bombs planted by terrorists in time to save innocent lives.

FATAL VISION: In 1968, the famous astrologer Jeanne Dixon (right) was about to give a speech at the Ambassador Hotel in Los Angeles. As she passed through the kitchen to get to the room where she was scheduled to speak, she stopped suddenly and blurted, "This is the place where Robert Kennedy will be shot. I can see him being carried out with blood on his face." Her prediction came true not long afterward.

DEADLY HANG-UP: The famous poet William Blake quit his job the first day that he was apprenticed to William Rylands, England's foremost engraver. Blake, who was 14 at the time, quit because when he looked at his employer, he had a chilling vision of him hanging dead on a gallows. Twelve years later, the vision came true when Rylands was hanged for forgery.

BROKEN RECORD: Little Mickie Kennedy lived with his parents in Australia in the late 1940s. His first words were "Mummy dead and Daddy gone." For three years, he repeated this phrase over and over again, much to everyone's puzzlement and horror. On his parents' ninth wedding anniversary, Mickie's father murdered his mother. At the exact moment that his father was sentenced to death, Mickie stopped repeating the phrase, and suddenly, inexplicably, died.

123

SPIRITS, SPECTERS, AND PHANTOMS

THE SPIRIT OF THE LAW: In 1991, an appeals court in New York State officially declared a house (above) in Nyack, New York, to be haunted.

BEWITCHED: The Witch's Eye near Thann, France, is the only part of Englesbourg Castle that is still standing. It was used for years as a prison for persons accused of witchcraft.

STARSHIP: In 1647, after sailing from England, a ship loaded with colonists and their possessions disappeared and was never heard from again. One year later, as witnessed by earlier colonists, it appeared in the sky with astounding clarity. Henry Wadsworth Longfellow's poem, "The Phantom Ship," commemorates this event.

HAIL TO THE GHOSTS: Over the years, nearly a dozen ghosts have haunted the White House. Mary Todd Lincoln saw the ghost of Andrew Jackson, Harry Truman saw the ghost of Abraham Lincoln, and William Howard Taft saw the ghost of Abigail Adams.

HAUNTED HIGHWAY: From 1984 to 1990 there were 519 car accidents on a 40-mile stretch of Alabama highway (above). Locals believe that the road is haunted by the ghosts of the Native Americans who are buried there.

GHOSTLY HIGH JINKS: The students at Burnley School of Professional Art in Seattle, Washington, have grown accustomed to seeing some unusual sights—desks that appear to be moving under their own steam, locked doors that mysteriously open by themselves, sounds of footsteps on vacant staircases. Who could be responsible? The ghosts of students past?

HOW BIZARRE!

BINDING PUNISHMENT: The book containing the transcript of the 1828 trial in which William Corder was convicted of murder is bound in his own skin. It can be seen in Moyses Hall Museum, Bury Saint Edmunds, England.

COOL RECEPTION: In September of 1990, Imelda Marcos (below) threw a party in honor of her late husband's 73rd birthday. The former president of the Philippines attended, but was not very good company, since he arrived frozen in a casket.

DON'T LEAVE HOME WITHOUT IT: Victorian vampire prevention kits (above) were sold in the 19th century. Each kit had everything you'd need to survive a Transylvanian vacation—a garlic necklace, a small vial of holy water, a wooden stake, and a crucifix-shaped gun that actually fired silver bullets.

NOVEL PREDICTION: In his 1898 novel, Morgan Robertson unknowingly predicted the sinking of the *Titanic*, 16 years before it was built. In his story, an 800-foot-long ocean liner, carrying 3,000 passengers, struck an iceberg on its maiden voyage one April night, and sank. Even the size and capacity of the *Titanic* matched Robertson's fictional ship, which was named the *Titan*.

TUNNEL VISION: The Tunnel of Posilipo in Naples, Italy, is 85 feet high, 22 feet wide, and one-half mile long. It is completely illuminated by the sun for only one day each year: at sunset on Halloween.

GRAVEYARD CRAFTS: In the 1700s, Honoré Fragonard, an anatomy teacher at one of the world's oldest veterinary schools, created bizarre objects out of animal and human cadavers (below). According to Christophe Degueurce, curator of the Fragonard Museum, Fragonard obtained cadavers from veterinary schools, human executions, medical schools, and even fresh graves. He stripped them of skin, dissected all the muscles and nerves, injected the blood vessels with wax, and steeped the bodies in alcohol for days. Finally he stretched them into elaborate poses and dried them with hot air. The finished objects were sought after by the very wealthy, among them, Louis XV. Examples of Fragonard's work can still be seen in the Fragonard Museum in France.

QUEEN OF HEARTS: Queen Marguerite de Valois of Navarre, Spain, had pockets sewn into the lining of her voluminous hoopskirt so she could always have with her the hearts of her 34 sweethearts. Each heart was embalmed and sealed in a separate box.

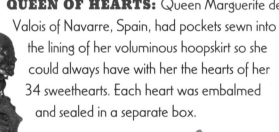

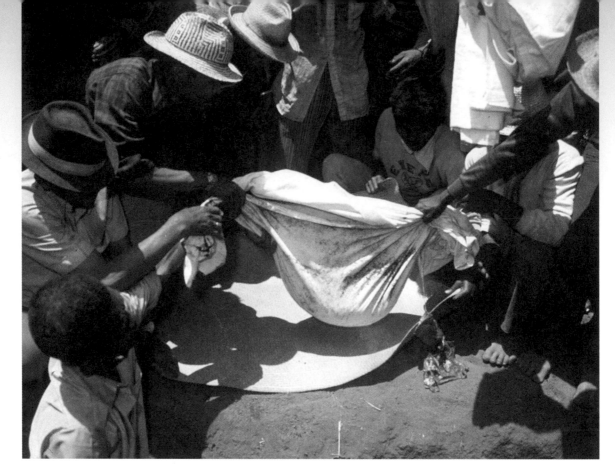

GRAVEYARD BASH: Madagascar, an island nation off the coast of South Africa, is home to nearly 15 million people who believe that honoring their dead loved ones with a sumptuous feast will bring the entire family good fortune. Every five years or so, families observe the holiday called Famadihana. The sacred ritual (above) begins when families remove their dead relatives from their tombs. Then they tell them the most important family news, and actually dance with the dead bodies—a practice that may seem shocking to outsiders, but actually helps the participants become less fearful of death. Everyone sits down to a lavish banquet. Afterward, the dead bodies are given new shrouds and placed back into their tombs.

DÉJÀ VU: *Barzai*, a book written by German novelist Ferdinand H. Grautoff in 1908, described a Japanese-American war in which unprepared American troops led by a fictional General MacArthur lost battles at first, but then rallied to defeat the Japanese—an eerie foreshadowing of actual events featuring the real General MacArthur (below), who led American troops to victory during World War II.

HOLY SMOKE SCREEN: The Dalai Lama (above), spiritual leader of Tibet, was held prisoner by the Chinese in his own palace. He planned his escape on the afternoon of March 17, 1959. Although Chinese troops surrounded the palace and huge searchlights were aimed at the building, the Dalai Lama and 80 companions slipped away under the cover of a sudden sandstorm.

BRIEF VISITATION: This photograph of Mary Todd Lincoln (above) was taken many years after Abraham Lincoln's death. So who is that standing behind her?

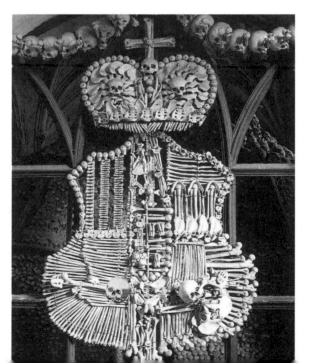

BONE-IFIED RETREAT: Six miles east of Prague in the Czech Republic, there is an 800-year-old chapel decorated entirely with bones (left). Bones are everywhere, giving the chapel a delicate, lacy appearance. A Czech woodcarver named Frantisek Rint, bedecked the chapel with the bones of 40,000 people because, as the story goes, the cemetery was filled, and many others were *dying* to be buried there.

GRAVEYARD LORE

DEAD BOLT: Lightning shattered the tombstone of T.G. Brownell, who was killed by a bolt of lightning.

SHORT AND SWEET EPITAPH: Here lies the body of Solomon Peas Under the daisies and under the trees. Peas is not here—only the pod; Peas shelled out; went home to God.

POP GOES THE CASKET: While on display in London, the casket of Queen Elizabeth I of England mysteriously exploded on the night before she was to be buried. The coffin was destroyed, yet the queen's body was unharmed.

YER OUT! In Chicago's Graceland Cemetery, the grave of William A. Hulbert, first president of the National League, is a stone baseball.

MOURNING PIGEON: Something strange marked the burial service for Captain Joseph Belain. As if in tribute to the man who had dedicated his life to saving the carrier pigeon from extinction, a carrier pigeon flew in from the sea, perched on the bier, and stayed until the service was over.

HOW TOUCHING! In Cornwall, England, there is a pet cemetery with a section devoted entirely to electronic Tamagotchi pets (right).

LEAD FOOT: Jonathan Blake's epitaph (right) is a cautionary tale for speeders.

HERE LIES
THE BODY OF
JONATHAN
BLAKE
STEPPED ON
THE GAS
INSTEAD OF
THE BRAKE.

SPECIAL EFFECTS: A few years after the death of Smith Treadwell, an exact likeness of him appeared on his gravestone.

MARY MAY

OH LORD,
SHE IS THIN

LOVING MOTHER

OOPS! A gravestone in Cooperstown, New York, was supposed to read: "Oh Lord, She Is Thine," but the stonecutter ran out of room.

DID YOU KNOW . . .

. . . that palm reading is called chiromancy?

. . . that in 1978, psychic Hubert Pearce guessed every card in the ESP tests given by Dr. Rhine at Duke University?

. . . that in 1908, astrologer John Hazelrigg predicted that presidents elected in the years 1920 (Warren G. Harding), 1940 (Franklin D. Roosevelt), and 1960 (John F. Kennedy), would die during their terms in office?

. . . that in England, a black cat crossing your path will bring you good fortune, while a white cat means bad luck?

. . . that the famous psychic Edgar Cayce, who never graduated from high school, was able to diagnose and treat the sick when he was in a trance?

. . . that the crystal ball was invented not by a psychic but by a mathematician? His name was John Dee, and he was the president of Manchester College in England in the mid-1500s.

JINXED!

CAR TROUBLE: On his way to Salinas, California, movie star James Dean was driving 80 miles per hour when he was killed in a head-on collision. Investigators were puzzled by evidence that suggested that Dean, who was an expert driver, had done nothing to avoid the crash. But that's not the end of the story.

Fans who flocked to the grisly scene were injured as they tried to remove pieces of the wreckage. A garage mechanic, hired to restore the sports car, broke both legs when it fell on him. After they bought parts from the car and installed them in their own race cars, one doctor was killed and another seriously injured. The two undamaged tires were sold to a man who had to be hospitalized after they both blew out at the same time.

The California Highway patrol planned to use the remains of the car in an auto show, but the night before the show opened, a fire broke out, destroying every vehicle but Dean's car, which escaped unscathed. The car was once again bound for Salinas when the driver lost control of the truck that was carrying it. The driver was killed instantly. Dean's car rolled off the truck. The next effort to display the car also ended in calamity, when the car, which had been welded back together, inexplicably broke into eleven pieces. The Florida police arranged to take the car for a safety display. But after the pieces of the car were crated and loaded onto a truck, the car disappeared, never to be seen again.

Puzzling but True

Robert Ripley's cartoons are filled with brainteasers, number fun, and quirky historical facts. Ripley actually made history in 1929 when he published a cartoon with the caption: "Believe It or Not, America has no national anthem." Public outcry in response to this cartoon was directly responsible for Congress adopting "The Star-Spangled Banner" as our official national anthem.

Believe It!

NOTABLE NUMBERS

WRITTEN IN THE CARDS: Mr. and Mrs. Joseph Meyerberg of Brooklyn, New York, discovered after their marriage that the number on her Social Security card was 064-01-8089, and the number on his was 064-01-8090.

LICENSE TO CLONE: Entirely by chance, identical license plates were issued to Stanley Golucki of Chicago, Illinois, in 1971 and 1972.

DON'T BANK ON IT! Karen Powell of Grandview, Washington, was assigned, by chance, bank account number 38-9-14999-8, which is the same as her Social Security number 389-14-9998.

LONG SHELF-LIFE: Could you arrange 15 books into all of their possible combinations? If you made one change per minute, it would take you 2,487,996 years to do it.

FORGET ABOUT IT! For a tossed coin to fall heads 50 times in a row, it would require one million people tossing ten coins a minute for 40 hours a week—and then it would occur only once every nine centuries.

UNLUCKY SPLIT: King Olaf of Norway and King Olof of Sweden rolled dice to decide ownership of the Island of Hisingen. Both threw double sixes, six times in a row. The Norwegian king finally threw down the dice with such force that one die split in two, and Hisingen has been Swedish ever since.

UNLUCKY NUMBER: The French dictator Napoleon Bonaparte used to spell his name with a _u_ (Buonaparte). According to numerology experts, it was right after he dropped that letter, leaving nine in his name, that his luck took a turn for the worse.

MENTAL BLOCKS: All the people in the world working day and night for a million years could not arrange these five six-sided letter blocks (above) into all of their possible combinations.

BEHIND THE EIGHT BALL: President José María Reina Barrios of Guatemala was assassinated at 8:00 P.M. on February 8, 1898, at No. 8 on 8th Street with a .38 caliber revolver. His assassin was shot 8 times.

SPREADING THE NEWS: If everyone who was told about a midnight murder told two other people within 12 minutes, everybody on Earth would know about it before morning.

PRESIDENTIAL STUMPER: In 1926, a Believe It or Not! cartoon carried the following question: If a bottle and a cork cost $1.05 and the bottle costs $1.00 more than the cork, what would be the cost of the cork? A few days later, the *Globe* received a letter from the White House inquiring what the answer was. In case you haven't figured it out already, the answer is at the bottom of the page.

WORKS EVERY TIME: Below are six sets of numbers with three columns in each set. To determine the age of anyone, ask that person to indicate which sets of figures contain his or her age. Then simply add up the upper left-hand figures in each of those sets and you will have the correct answer.

8	27	46		1	23	45		16	27	54
9	28	47		3	25	47		17	28	55
10	29	56		5	27	49		18	29	56
11	30	57		7	29	51		19	30	57
12	31	58		9	31	53		20	31	58
13	40	59		11	33	55		21	48	59
14	41	60		13	35	57		22	49	60
15	42	61		15	37	59		23	50	61
24	43	62		17	39	61		24	51	62
25	44	63		19	41	63		25	52	63
26	45			21	43			26	53	

4	23	46		32	43	54		2	23	46
5	28	47		33	44	55		3	26	47
6	29	52		34	45	56		6	27	50
7	30	53		35	46	57		7	30	51
12	31	54		36	47	58		10	31	54
13	36	55		37	48	59		11	34	55
14	37	60		38	49	60		14	35	58
15	38	61		39	50	61		15	38	59
20	39	62		40	51	62		18	39	62
21	44	63		41	52	63		19	42	63
22	45			42	53			22	43	

ELECTION LORE

HIGH STAKES: In New Mexico, when a race is too close to call, the candidates play poker to decide the winner. The last time this happened was in 1999. Democrat Lena Milligan and Republican Jim Blanq played a hand of five-card stud (left). Blanq won, earning himself the title of magistrate judge.

ELECTION LUNACY: The 2000 presidential election wasn't the only one that seemed to drag on indefinitely. The 1876 race between Rutherford B. Hayes and Samuel Tilden depended on a recount in several states. One county sent duplicate sets of ballots—one real and one fake. It's a good thing, too, since the fake set was, indeed, hijacked. Both campaigns seemed to suffer from a lack of fair play, including stuffing ballot boxes to the extent that in some cases the votes actually exceeded the population!

STOGIE STATS: The first polls to determine the popularity of presidential candidates were conducted in the late 1800s by putting the candidates' pictures on cigar boxes and then noting which sold the best.

LOUSY CHOICE: In 19th-century Sweden, a new burgomaster was chosen by placing a louse in the center of a table. The man whose beard the insect jumped into held the office for the next year.

AGAINST ALL ODDS: Governor Mel Carnahan (below) of Missouri was killed in a plane crash a month before the 2000 election. But that did not stop him from defeating his opponent. Because Carnahan's death was so close to the election, his name remained on the ballot in which he was running for the Senate. The senator's wife, Jean Carnahan, will serve as senator in his place.

LINCOLN AND KENNEDY

Two of America's greatest and most beloved presidents are linked by an eerie set of coincidences. A pattern runs through the circumstances of their presidencies and brutal assassinations that hints at some unknown, unexplained connection.

- Both Kennedy and Lincoln were deeply involved in the civil rights issue of his era. In Lincoln's time, the issue was slavery; in Kennedy's, it was segregation.

- Lincoln's assassin, John Wilkes Booth, was born in 1839.

- Kennedy's assassin, Lee Harvey Oswald, was born in 1939.

- Lincoln had a secretary named Kennedy who warned him not to go to the theater that night.

- Kennedy had a secretary named Lincoln who warned him not to go to Dallas.

- Both were shot on a Friday.

- Both were shot from behind.

- Both wives were present when their husbands were shot.

- Booth shot Lincoln in a theater and ran into a warehouse.

- Oswald shot Kennedy from a warehouse and ran into a theater.

- Both presidents were succeeded by men named Johnson.

- Both Johnsons were Democrats from the South.

- The Johnson who succeeded Lincoln was born in 1808. The Johnson who succeeded Kennedy was born in 1908.

- Both presidents' last names have seven letters. Their successors' first and last names combined have 13 letters, and the combined letters in the names of their assassins' first and last names have 15.

137

WEIRD LAW

PUTTING A BITE INTO CRIME: In Oklahoma, it's against the law to take a bite out of someone else's hamburger.

SEEING PINK: Pink was the favorite color of Empress Elizabeth of Russia, daughter of Peter the Great. During her reign from 1761 to 1762, she issued a decree that any other woman who wore that color would be put to death.

BUS-TED! In Indiana, it's against the law for people to travel on a bus within four hours of eating garlic.

CLASSIFIED MATERIAL: For 3,000 years, the secret of making silk was known only to the Chinese. Anyone who revealed it to a foreigner would be put to death.

DRESS CODE FOR DUMMIES: In New York City, it's against the law to leave a naked dummy in a shop window.

LIES OR CONSEQUENCES: Russian Czar Paul I made it a crime for anyone to mention his baldness in his presence. The punishment was death by flogging.

BE KIND TO MONSTERS: The White River Monster Sanctuary in Newport, Arkansas, was created by the state's legislature, which made it illegal to "molest, kill, or trample" a legendary sea monster.

GUILT TRIP: In 1650, Oswald Kröl of Lindau, Germany, was convicted and executed for murder. Kröl was later vindicated. From that day on, his skeleton was propped up before the jurist who had pronounced the death sentence.

TWISTED HISTORY

PEDAL-PUSHER: Edith Wilson, wife of United States President Woodrow Wilson, often rode a bicycle in the corridors of the White House.

YOUR ROYAL STEEDSHIP: The Roman Emperor Caligula is remembered as The Horse Emperor because he bestowed the rank of Consul and Co-Regent upon his favorite horse, Incitatus. The horse was given every honor of the office and was provided with an ivory manger and a gold drinking goblet from which it drank wine.

MAKING HIS "POINT": Dwight D. Eisenhower (below), who became one of the most successful commanders in history, was admitted to West Point in 1911 only because the applicant who ranked ahead of him in the entrance exam flunked the physical.

GRANDFATHER OF OUR COUNTRY: George Washington was not really the first president of the United States—John Hanson was. In 1781, Maryland finally signed the Articles of Confederation, and the union of the original 13 colonies became an actuality. The man who signed for Maryland was the elected president of the United States in the assembled Congress. On the occasion of his victory at Yorktown, Washington addressed Hanson as president of the United States.

DYING TO RULE: Peter III of Russia was murdered in 1762 at the age of 34. He was crowned 34 years after his death. His coffin had to be opened so that the crown could be placed on his head.

STRANGER THAN FICTION

FEATHERBRAINED: If Benjamin Franklin had had his way, our national bird would be a turkey instead of a bald eagle.

DEAD MEN DON'T ADVERTISE: Neb Jesse Boorn of Manchester, Vermont, was convicted of murdering his brother-in-law. Boorn was freed when an ad placed by the brother-in-law in the *Rutland Herald* in November of 1819 proved that he was alive and living in Dover.

KIDNAP-PROOF: When Sultan Aboul Hamid I was six, he was imprisoned in a small cage. He was not allowed to leave it until he was enthroned as ruler of the Turkish Empire, 43 years later.

SUCH A HEADACHE! In 1867, William Thompson of Omaha, Nebraska, was shot by Native Americans of the Cheyenne tribe. Thinking he was dead, they removed part of his scalp. Imagine their surprise when Thompson regained consciousness, grabbed his scalp, and ran. He later donated it to the Omaha Public Library.

FULL STOMACH, EMPTY HEAD: In 1792, during the French Revolution, King Louis XVI was fleeing from bloodthirsty mobs when he slipped away to eat at an inn in Vincennes. He paid for his meal with a gold coin bearing his own likeness. The innkeeper recognized the king at once and notified the king's enemies. Louis was dragged back to Paris where he and his wife, Marie Antoinette, were beheaded.

THE LEGACY

In a strange and bizarre twist of fate he would have appreciated, Ripley collapsed in 1949 while making the 13th episode of his new weekly television series. The segment he had been taping was a dramatized sequence on the origin of "Taps"—a hauntingly sad tune played at military funerals. Ripley is buried in his hometown of Santa Rosa, California, in a place called Oddfellows Cemetery. Ripley's name lives on in the Odditoriums that can be found in cities around the world, in the cartoons that are still being created, and in the Ripley website at www.ripleys.com where new BIONs are printed daily. Perhaps some day your story will appear in one of them. As long as there exists a keen interest in the seemingly unbelievable, the Ripley legacy will never die.

WE'D LOVE TO BELIEVE YOU!

Do you have a Believe It or Not! story that has happened to you or to someone you know? If it's weird enough and if you would like to share it, the people at Ripley's would love to hear about it. You can send your Believe It or Not! entries to:

The Director of the Archives
Ripley Entertainment
5728 Major Boulevard
Orlando, Florida 32819

INDEX

ACKNOWLEDGMENTS Nancy Hall, Inc. and the author would like to thank the following for their invaluable contributions: RIPLEY ENTERTAINMENT, especially Bob Masterson, Norm Deska, Bob Whiteman, Edward Meyer, Lisa McCalla, and Christy Barnes; SIGNATURES NETWORK, especially Dell Furano, Karine Versace, Chris Guirlinger, Gladys Ng Blumin, and Vicki Pedersen; SCHOLASTIC INC, especially Ellie Berger, Craig Walker, Tonya Martin, Maria Barbo, Joan Moloney, Charles Carmony, and Isabelle Hershkowitz.

PHOTO CREDITS Ripley Entertainment and the editors of this book wish to thank the following photographers, agents, and other individuals for permission to use and reprint the following photographs in this book. Any photographs included in this book that are not acknowledged below are property of the Ripley Archives. Great effort has been made to obtain permission from the owners of all materials included in this book. Any errors that may have been made are unintentional and will gladly be corrected in future printings if notice is sent to Ripley Entertainment, 5728 Major Boulevard, Orlando, Florida 32819.

10 Jackie Mitchell/National Baseball Hall of Fame Library, Cooperstown, NY/copyright unknown
10 Babe Ruth/National Baseball Hall of Fame Library, Cooperstown, NY
11 Henry Armstrong/Library of Congress, Prints and Photographs Division, Carl Van Vechten collection, LC-USZ62-114433 DLC
12 Wilma Rudolph/Tennessee State Library & Archives/Paul Schleicher/Copyright unknown
14 Roller Man/Christophe Lebedinsky
14 Wim Hof/Henny Boogert
14 Sky Tennis/Tony Hathaway
16 Derek Jeter/2000 Rich Pilling/MLB Photos
16 Tao Berman/Brandon Knapp/Pickanimage.com
19 Meteor/Corel Corporation
19 Moon/Corel Corporation
20 Lightning/CORBIS
22 Padaung Images/CORBIS
23 Sea Urchin/CORBIS
28 Clock/Laura Miller
32 Elizabeth Christensen/Atlantic Syndication
37 Tom Thumb/National Museum of American History, Smithsonian Institution
38 Mozart/Library of Congress, Prints and Photographs Division, Detroit Publishing Company Collection
42 Remote-control Surgery/Dr. Douglas Boyd
43 Leech/Courtesy of Leeches USA Ltd.
43 Bee/PhotoDisc
44 Komodo Dragon/Galen R. Frysinger
46 Coconut Tree Climber/Tony Arruza/CORBIS
46 Julia "Butterfly" Hill/Shaun Walker/OtterMedia.com
47 Les Echassiers/Clément Allard
49 Howard Hughes/Associated Press
53 Gene Pool/Gary Sutton
54 Bagel/Laura Miller
54 Pretzel/Laura Miller
56 InsectNside/Courtesy of HotLix
58 Koala Bear/Corel Corporation
59 Klipspringer Antelope/PhotoDisc
59 Hummingbird/Frank Lane Picture Agency/CORBIS
59 Prairie Dogs/W. Perry Conway/CORBIS
60 Fawn/Corel Corporation
60 Alex the Parrot/William Munoz
60 Mangabey/Samantha Smith/Yerkes Regional Primate Research Center
61 Vampire Bat/Gary Braasch/CORBIS

64 Twinky, the Miniature Horse/Lisa Carpenter
65 Endal and Allen Parton/Courtesy Veronica Morgan, Canine Partners for Independence, www.cpiuk.org
66 Lulu the Pig/AP Photo/Shawn Baldwin
70 Wolf Fish/Peter Auster and Paul Donaldson, National Undersea Research Center—University of Connecticut
70 Starfish/PhotoDisc
71 Hermit Crab/Corel Corporation
74 Water Spider/David Glynne Fox
74 Hercules Beetle/Jason D. Weintraub/Aurelian Entographics
76 Lava/Corel Corporation
76 Mt. Pelee Survivor/Rykoff Collection/CORBIS
77 Beaver/PhotoDisc
78 Dolphin/CORBIS
78 Lusitania/Bettmann/CORBIS
81 Mel Gibson/Rogers & Cowan
82 Vesna Vulovic/Associated Press
83 Air India Crash/Associated Press
84 Rodney Fox/Courtesy of Rodney Fox
87 Sarah Donohue/David Williams
90 Dan Kish/John Ker/HI-TORQUE Publications, Inc.
92 Pineapple House/The Landmark Trust, 802-245-6868 in the U.S.
93 Bottle House/Courtesy Réjeanne Arsenault
94 Color-by-Number House/Mark Van Noppen
95 Stuyvesant Apartments/Library of Congress, Prints and Photographs Division, Historic American Buildings Survey, HABS, NY, 31-NEYO, 25-1
96 Bostonian Hotel/Reprinted with permission from the Millennium Bostonian
96 Ice Hotel/Fredric Alm, Courtesy of the Ice Hotel
97 Jules' Undersea Lodge/Courtesy Jules' Undersea Lodge, Key Largo, FL
97 Sveti Stefan (St. Stephen)/Galen R. Frysinger
98 Skydome/Corel Corporation
98 Armour-Stiner House/Historic American Buildings Survey, National Park Service, HABS No. NY-5620-11, Jack Boucher, 1978
99 National Fresh Water Fishing Hall of Fame/Courtesy National Fresh Water Fishing Hall of Fame
100 Reykjavik/Corel Corporation
100 Giant Buddha/Julia Waterlow;

EyeUbiquitous/CORBIS
101 Snake Dinner/Corel Corporation
102 Guadix, Spain/Peter Hill & Linda Pan
102 Cappadocia/Corel Corporation
109 Willard Wigan/Art International Management
109 Miniature Snow White Sculpture/Art International Management
113 George Vlosich/Courtesy of George Vlosich, Sr.
113 Etch A Sketch Portrait/Courtesy of George Vlosich, Sr.
113 Pocheptsov Painting/Courtesy of the Pocheptsov family
113 Georgie Pocheptsov/Courtesy of the Pocheptsov family
115 Thomas Edison/Denver Public Library, Western History Collection; Photo by Harry Rhoads, Call# Rh-863
116 Bicycle Stained-Glass Window/Frank T. Bowater
118 Katrina Mumaw/William Edwards Photography
118 Kris Holm/Ryan Leech
120 Archduke Ferdinand/Bettmann/CORBIS
122 Chris Robinson/Courtesy of Chris Robinson
123 Jeanne Dixon/Associated Press UNIVERSAL PRESS SYNDICATE
124 NY Haunted House/Mark Kavanaugh
125 Alabama Highway/Milton Fullman
126 Imelda Marcos/Bettmann/CORBIS
127 Fragonard Object/C. Degueurce
128 Madagascar Festival/AP Photo/Toussaint Raharison
128 MacArthur and Troops/Associated Press
129 Dalai Lama/Galen Rowell/CORBIS
129 Mary Todd Lincoln/The Lloyd Ostendorf Collection
129 Bone Church/Ben Fraser
130 Tamagotchi pets/Laura Miller
134 Napoleon/Austrian Archives/CORBIS
135 Letter Blocks/Laura Miller
136 Poker Game/Zeno Kiehne/The Messenger
137 John F. Kennedy/Photo No. ST-C237-1-63 in the John F. Kennedy Library
137 Abraham Lincoln/Library of Congress, Prints and Photographs Division, LC-USZ62-13016 DLC
137 Governor Mel Carnahan/Governor's Press Office
138 Hamburger/Laura Miller
139 Dwight D. Eisenhower/The Dwight D. Eisenhower Library

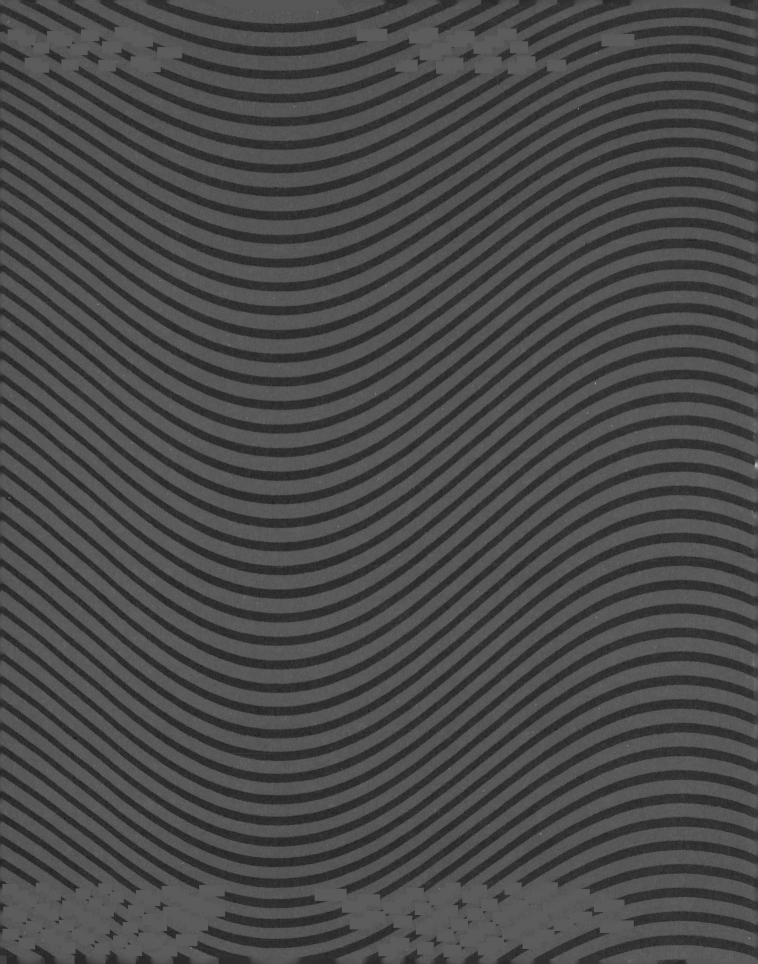